CW00460600

THE MULE ... MILITARY SERVICE

THE MULE IN
MILITARY SERVICE

A proud record in the British and Indian armies

Anthony Clayton

The Book Guild Ltd

First published in Great Britain in 2017 by
The Book Guild Ltd
9 Priory Business Park
Wistow Road, Kibworth
Leicestershire, LE8 0RX
Freephone: 0800 999 2982
www.bookguild.co.uk
Email: info@bookguild.co.uk
Twitter: @bookguild

Cover image 'Animals in War Memorial' Park Lane, London
used by kind permission of David Backhouse

Typeset in Minion Pro

Printed and bound in Great Britain by CPI Group (UK) Ltd, Croydon, CR0 4YY

ISBN 978 1912083 664

British Library Cataloguing in Publication Data.
A catalogue record for this book is available from the British Library.

Animals have played an important role over my eighty-seven years of life. This work about one animal, generally overlooked, is an expression of my gratitude to them all.

Contents

List of Illustrations

As me and my companions were scrambling up a hill,
The path was lost in rolling stones, but we went forward still;
For we can wriggle and climb, my lads, and turn up everywhere,
And it's our delight on a mountain height, with a leg or two to
    spare!

Good luck to every sergeant, then, that lets us pick our road;
Bad luck to all the driver-men that cannot pack a load:
For we can wriggle and climb, my lads, and turn up everywhere,
And it's our delight on a mountain height, with a leg or two to
    spare!

Rudyard Kipling, "Parade Song of the Camp-Animals"
Chapter 7, "Her Majesty's Servants", *The Jungle Book*

Acknowledgements

A large part of this work is based upon a very full, unpublished manuscript – *The Military Mule in the British and Indian Army: An Anthology* – put together and in part written by Brian Nicholls. The manuscript contains a rich collection of personal experiences, memories and details of the service of mules from individual officers with much specialist knowledge relating to the handling of mules in many events and campaigns. With the kind permission of Brian Nicholls, I have drawn freely on material in the manuscript which falls into three parts:

Part 1 – "Over Two Hundred Years of Valuable Service" by Brian Nicholls.

Part 2 – "The Indian Army Transport Mule" by the late Major Philip Malins.

Part 3 – "The Mountain Artillery Mule" by the late Lieut-Colonel Charles McFetridge.

Without these records, this book could not have been written. The manuscript is now back in the hands of the British Mule Society from where Ruth Bickford also provided me with useful articles from past issues of the Society's journal, *The Mule*.

A bibliography of published sources on which I have drawn can be found at the end of this work. Some works carry full details of campaigns, others one or two paragraphs, many just providing an interesting sentence. Some are modern, some are old. It was only in a book published in 1873 that I was able to find anything at all about mules at Waterloo. The works listed are all in the library of the Royal Military Academy Sandhurst and I am greatly indebted to the librarian Andrew Orgill and Ken Franklin of the library staff for all their help.

These two major centres of source material complement each other, mine is the string that seeks to bind them into the wider context of British and Indian military history. It has been a privilege to write.

For much help with the illustrations I am especially grateful to David Backhouse for the front cover photograph and also for other photographs following research undertaken for me by Neera Puttapitat of the Imperial War Museum. Lucy Gosling of the Mary Evans Photograph Library, Brigadier Martin Skipworth of the Royal Signals Museum and Robin Braysher of the Salonika Campaign Society.

Four friends have helped me greatly in my research and writing; John Card for much-needed communication technical assistance, Julie Card for converting my untidy handwriting into a neat typescript, Dr H.P. Willmott for general advice and help with transport from my house to Sandhurst and Dr Walter Bowring for musical memories of a mountain battery in Italy. My warmest thanks to all of them.

1

Introduction: Mules and War

For over 200 years a very ordinary looking animal, the mule, has appeared, almost always very willingly, to play a vital role in world wars and many local campaigns in support of British Army-led formations and units. Even in this age of helicopter and motor transport, supply calls are still made for the mule with its sure feet on unsure ground, stamina and resistance to disease.

The British Army was founded in 1661, after the Restoration. It is possible that mules were used by the Duke of Marlborough in his campaigns, in the 18th century North American wars and the Bengal Army in India, but draught horses, oxen and bullocks seem more likely. For certain though is the fact that mules and donkeys have provided a transport service in campaigns heavily dependent on their delivery of guns, food, ammunition, tentage and clothing with also casualty evacuation, from Wellington's Peninsula campaign to the late 20th century operations in Bosnia Herzegovina in 1995.

Little credit in military history writing has been given to their work. The word "mule" in the 21st century too often pejoratively connotes a perverse, irrational, "mulish" obstinacy, a perception seemingly self-perpetuating and ongoing. For some, also, the mule has been jeered at as illegitimate, not a natural species, being unable to reproduce itself and therefore not deserving the same attention and respect as that given to other animals, horses, camels, oxen or elephants. Within this psychological contamination, the mule has been exposed to a form of species discrimination and reduced to an underclass. While other more eye-catching animals are the lead actors, the mule is just a stage-hand, an uninteresting animal whose presence is an unavoidable necessity, an "other" rather than a team member. With the honourable exception of the mule's friends and admirers, there still remains little interest in the mule and the role played by them as one of mankind's most useful animals and an "unsung hero" in many campaigns and wars is passed over.

This work, primarily about mules, also records donkeys in military service. These, the males called Jack Assess and the females Jennets are an old Asian species, distinct from the traditional European donkey to be seen at the seaside, being larger and of greater stamina. Their value came to be appreciated in the late 18th century. George Washington and others who were despatching Jacks and Jennets to the United States, were mating Jacks with mares and founded the massive American mule breeding industry. This was essential in a country with no railways and few roads at the time, and one to be copied in due course by Argentina and Uruguay, as well as Spain in Europe.

The mules so bred were, and still are with very few exceptions, sterile, having inherited an odd-number chromosome group. In compensation, mules have a special "hybrid vigour", ensuring a constant demand for their services for over 150 years. Quite often the Jack Ass donkey carried a slightly superior general public cachet and was better cared for. But in a number of cases histories have simply presented combined "mules and donkeys" totals or lumped them both together as "other animals" after figures for horses. Photographs wrongly captioned appear in several books. Where combined mules and donkeys totals appear the majority would usually have been mules.

In colour mules may vary from very dark brown to chestnut or a very attractive light beige. Some may have white marking patches. Different national breeds of mules can vary greatly, American Missouri mules being especially large and strong. More average European, Asian and North African mules can range between 700 and 1400lbs in weight and between 4½ and 5½ feet in technical terms 13.2 to 16.2 "hands" in height. Mules can be distinguished from Jack donkeys by their slightly larger size, thicker body-build and smaller hooves. The particular feature of the mule is that, moving forward with his head well down, the mule can see and at once coordinate all four legs, so making himself extremely safe in his footfall along narrow paths and tracks. Numerous cases have been recorded where mules have correctly and wisely refused to follow a particular pathway. Smaller mules are better for individual riders or human passengers and loads of up to 150 occasionally 200lbs; larger mules can carry even heavier pack-loads over 400lbs or work in draught teams for cart pulling. Mules become most useful for military transport when they are between three and eight years old, at their peak between four and six, but remaining useful for a further ten years. After the age of three mules may become difficult to break in and train. For some of the very heavy artillery loadings, larger and more mature mules up to the age of eleven or twelve were sometimes preferred with some trusted and faithful mules still serving in their thirties. Further, mules costed substantially less than horses, lived a longer working life and were cheaper to feed, requiring less grain. A tough digestive system enabled mules to break down and digest new, hitherto inedible vegetation and extract moisture in otherwise dry and inhospitable country.

There is also a third animal, the hinny, the offspring of a male horse and a female donkey. Hinnies have shorter ears and stronger legs than a mule and are slightly smaller than most mules. Many have grey-blue coats. They appear occasionally on battlefields but do not have the same stamina as a mule.

Mules could, and very often did, suffer from cruelty at times wanton from breeders, dealers, owners and handler muleteers. These latter could vary very considerably, in different campaigns often reflecting the handling and experience of the military command or contract muleteer personnel. Some mules would have been broken in by rough rope training work before being sent to the market, others might have had to wait until they had been bought or requisitioned for military service to "learn on the job". It was held by some that female mules were easier to manage than males, and many male mules were gelded. One advantage of a donkey who was carefully trained was that the smaller size enabled it to work in very small confined spaces such as a hospital tent from which, after delivering a casualty, they could exit without having to turn round; their perceived disadvantage was the smaller loads that they could carry.

Some mule markets were local and near to a campaign headquarters at the start of a campaign. But more often, the military mule would have been purchased for duties far from his home environment and, over the centuries, have had to experience a sea passage to the theatre of operations. Whether in the age of sail or steam such a journey, short or long, would have been unlikely to be comfortable. Mules would be crowded in pens on ships' decks for short journeys, or packed closely in ships' holds; food and water supply was often limited and loading and unloading mules on board and to shore usually meant slings and ropes. In rough weather frightened mules would panic, attempt to stampede, break rope fastenings, kick out at sailors. Some might have to be destroyed either by shooting, throat slitting or simply by being thrown overboard. Where ventilation was poor mules would fall victim to "shipping fever", a shortness of breath respiratory illness. In more modern times the conditions for mules packed into cattle trains or in the backs of lorries could be equally severe. The mule is a clean animal and does not like standing on a floor or ground in its own mess, and or any other dirt.

On arrival at the scene of operations mules would be selected according to size, fitness and training, together with the military needs of the moment for pack-load carrying or cart pulling duties. A few would carry people, more often on return journey when mules would carry the sick and injured, sometimes with a cavalry escort for protection. Many of the best mules came to be selected for elite mountain artillery batteries. Officially, all mules were given a number, recorded on the hoof, or in later procedures by burning the number on the neck, but in campaigns where large numbers of mules were needed in a hurry this was not always the practice. Nor could it be in campaigns where local people either willingly or unwillingly provided mules, sometimes with their owners as muleteers.

On the journeys much would depend on the relationship between the individual mule and the muleteer in charge of the team or group within the section of a mule train, and also upon the length of daily or nightly journeys and the conditions in which the journeys were being made. In the 1809–1812 Peninsula Campaign, for example, the journey, if not broken by change-over stops, could be as long as 400 miles – twelve to fourteen miles per day for a working mule. But at Gallipoli in 1915 or Burma in 1942–45, the length of journey might be much shorter or longer, in conditions of climate and terrain that was more difficult. The daily diet for the maximum efficiency of a mule was, and still is, 14 pounds of hay and 9 pounds of oats, corn or barley. Forage for the mule in campaign supply trains or columns was almost as important a factor as the supplies for a fighting man.

On the road the best mules would be directed by stick or whip in light touches; if reluctant, they might be roped

5

and dragged forward by muleteers or soldiers, or be pushed from behind. Mule carts, in any and all campaigns could vary in size and reliability. In difficult terrain, in particular steep slopes, carts could break free and run down backwards onto any following mules, or if the ropes held drag the mules backwards. Or, again, a cart might roll forward, pushing the mule into danger and perhaps death. For such reasons many field commanders preferred pack-mules to carts as being less likely that a frightened mule would cause traffic chaos. Speeds of mule columns and trains varied according to the terrain, but 2½ miles per hour was generally used as planning basis with daily journeys lengths depending upon terrain, climate, daylight and enemy action but usually forty to fifty miles with often a night's rest, the same day after day.

A trained experienced muleteer could, with quiet, firm handling, draw upon all that was and remains best in a mule, above all the sheer stamina and acceptance of heat, wind, rain, blizzards, ice and snow, even when icicles might be hanging from noses. Facing a hillside, a mule could often select the best route across. Mules are also good swimmers. The mules' loyalty, patience and toleration of grim conditions, even under bombardment, soon came to command respect, even general affection. Individual mules, and each with his own personality, came to inspire muleteers with a personal bonding and were given names; some became unit or sub-unit mascots. In return a well-cared-for mule gave a personal loyalty to his muleteer.

Mules are semi-domesticated and intelligent animals with a mischievous sense of humour, sentient to their environment, quick to recognise a change in a muleteer's non-verbal communication and body language, and with a remarkable ability to sense danger. Some accounts suggest that mules could pass on to each other warning signs if an approaching muleteer was likely to be bringing misfortune, either personally or in the context of operations. Many Indian Army muleteers, at the end of a day's march, would lie down and quietly sing to their mules, receiving a warm nuzzle in return, and many cases exist where a mule, believing his master was in danger, would rush to try to help. In several operations medical officers have commented that mules carrying the wounded or sick seemed to have a sense of special responsibility and need for care on the march. A "shared experience" sense among a small team or group of mules could lead to a willingness to follow a team leader mule selected by the muleteer, the chosen leader might be given a bell or some form of rattle for others to follow. The "shared experience" sense could also extend to the "putting at ease" of a new mule joining a well-cared-for team. The best muleteers appreciated that mules have much longer memories than horses or oxen, something that was often a surprise for the inexperienced.

Grief over the injury or the death of a mule was shared by other mules and muleteers alike. An inadequately trained muleteer or wantonly cruel muleteer could produce all that appeared negative in mules: bad temper, stubborn obstinacy, kicking out – the mule's natural self-defence – biting of ropes and rugs, refusal to move, lying down. Mule kicks were almost always well directed and very painful. Sometimes this behaviour was mischief, of which mules have a great sense, but it would lead a bad muleteer to explosions of temper, worse behaviour and cruelty. A very heavy bombardment or small arms fire, which mules particularly dislike, could lead to panic. On some occasions, happily few over the years, a stampede might follow. All mules reacted to noisy loads such as cooking kettles, meat and to dead bodies, and wise muleteers would clear any corpses away from tracks in advance of a mule column. But in some campaigns a withdrawing enemy army would deliberately leave corpses of mules or muleteers to delay an opponent's advance.

A further, theoretical and as yet unproven, point concerning the psychology of mules merits mention. Some theorists argue that mules are aware subconsciously that they are not fully natural animals and that they cannot reproduce. Theorists also argue that mules have an awareness, perhaps from witnessing that other animals were being whipped less and were generally receiving better treatment than they were, which was often the case in campaigns where horses appeared alongside mules, that they were in the end expendable. Such perception is claimed by some as explanation for refractory mule behaviour and suggests an individual reasoning capability. Some incidents suggest the mule, with its hybrid vigour input, can think beyond the minute. These are interesting lines of thought but ones that, at present, much remain conjectural.

Care, and of course food and water were vital parts of the duties of a good muleteer. It was essential that packs when loaded had to be carefully balanced; a badly loaded mule would soon suffer and protest. At the end of a day's march the quick removal of the load and loosening of a mule's ropes and harness to enable him to roll was important. Mules have tender mouths that can become very sore if a mule is suddenly pulled or dragged. Water in many campaigns needed checking for purity; mules themselves might reject water they sensed to be polluted. Mud and dirt had to be cleaned off hooves. All these tasks were essential for the animal's well being but have not always been carried out by lazy, ill-tempered, or simply exhausted muleteers. Mules' braying could add to exasperation. Two muleteers were generally needed for the grooming, daily when possible, of a mule: one to groom and one to control any kicking or biting, even putting a mule into wooden stocks while shoeing. In most campaigns shoeing might need attention, the duty of a unit's farrier, usually a sergeant and for many years the only member of the regimental battery with a responsibility for the health of mules. The nature and proximity of enemy forces might require that any noise, such as mules baying had to be stifled. Sick mules might have to be withdrawn to a special area to recover, evacuation to a veterinary section if one existed, or death. Any proper form of veterinary services for mules was not provided until the mid-19th century; real academic veterinary studies and teaching only developed in the second half of the century. An Army Veterinary Service had been formed as early as 1895 but the few men serving within it had very little professional knowledge and their priorities were almost invariably horses. Fully professional veterinary treatment with veterinary field hospitals only properly appeared in the 20th century. By the last years of the First World War, however, it was becoming more important to recruit a man capable of changing a sparking plug than ensuring that the pack of a mule was well balanced. The mule, useful but expendable, remained at the tail end of priorities until the Burma and Italian campaigns of the Second World War when, suddenly and unexpectedly, the mule came into his own.

2

The Peninsula Campaign and Waterloo

The wars against Napoleon, in particular the long 1808–1813 campaign of Sir Arthur Wellesley, later Duke of Wellington, in Portugal, Spain and Southern France, saw significant progress in military logistics, transport and administration. The campaign began with a defence of Portugal and was followed by a series of operations against very capably led French armies in Spain, the eventual ejection of the French from Spain and Wellington's entry into France.

For many years, the Army's practice had been one of very largely leaving regiments and battalions to make their own supply transport arrangements by hiring or purchasing draught horses or other animals in numbers governed by the wealth of each unit. The inadequacies of this system were simply overlooked. For the brief 1794–1795 expedition to the Netherlands, a corps of waggoners had been formed, but it achieved little and was disbanded. In 1799 a Royal Waggon Corps, a little later restyled as the Royal Waggon Train, incorporating an Irish Commissariat Waggon Corps, was formed, but too late to be of value to one of the initial operations: Sir John Moore's Corunna expedition.

From the start of the main Peninsula campaign, Wellington had of necessity a clear appreciation of his supply and transport needs and throughout the campaign his Commissariat organised Royal Waggon Trains. Several different animals were used in the trains, of these by far the most important was the mule, best suited to the mountains, hills, tracks and passes that had to be navigated and through regions where there were few resources for requisitioning.

War in the Iberian Peninsula had begun in November 1807 when a French Army had invaded Portugal and captured Lisbon. In March of the next year, the French invaded Spain where Napoleon installed his brother as king. The Royal Navy, controlling the seas, enabled Wellington to land at the head of a British force, including German and Portuguese soldiers, near Lisbon on 1st August 1808. Helped by a Portuguese national uprising he was able to defeat a French army in battle and force a French withdrawal from Portugal.

A second British landing on the Iberian Peninsula followed at the end of August when Moore, at the head of his force, landed on the north-west coast of Spain. Plans were prepared for columns from Portugal and Corunna to advance towards Valladolid in north-west Spain, and from there later move on to challenge French authority in Madrid. But a series of misfortunes – confused political and military direction, the non-arrival of much-needed Spanish help, and the assembly of a very large French army in Spain – necessitated an urgent withdrawal. The epic winter retreat back to Corunna remains a story of extreme hardship and suffering; dangerous and slippery snow and ice-covered mountain passes; inadequate and often total shortages of food, tentage, warm clothing and even blankets; and continuous French harassment. Very heavy casualties, including the death of Moore himself, were suffered before ragged survivors were evacuated by the Royal Navy. Accounts record dying and dead mules along the sides of tracks and paths. All suffered severely from the absence of shelter and forage, dying from natural causes. Further south, Wellington was forced to abandon Lisbon and retreat to fortified defence lines.

Four years of hard fighting across Portugal and Spain then followed. The French were never able to eject Wellington from Spain and Portugal, and Wellington was unable to force the French armies back into France until 1813 and 1814. Wellington's army increased in strength each year and continued to include Portuguese and German formations and units. In July 1809 Wellington's army totalled 30,000, of which 21,000 were British serving in thirty infantry battalions, whose strengths ranged from 300 to 900, artillery units of 3-pdr muzzle-loading guns and six cavalry regiments. By July 1812 Wellington's strength had increased to some 45,000 fighting effectives organised in four small divisions of different sizes. By early 1814 he was commanding seven infantry divisions more equal in size, together with an artillery division, a small light division and a complete Portuguese division. German and Portuguese men served in several of the other divisions. In total, including artillery gunners, engineers and logistic personnel, some 110,000 men crossed the Spanish-French frontier to enter France. In the foothills of the Pyrenees units of the Royal Artillery proudly styled themselves as mountain batteries.

The main component of the supply transport system was the mule, with its patience if well-managed and ability to work very hard but requiring relatively little food or water. The hiring or purchase of mules at the outset in 1808 and 1809 was, however, chaotic. Apart from a small number of mules brought from Ireland, locally bred animals had to be bought by the Commissariat from local dealers in the Lisbon markets. Most dealers had little concern for the welfare of mules and charged as much as they could get – between 50 and 90 dollars, at an administration and exchange rate of 5 shillings to the dollar. Purchases were made by the Commissariat for the waggon train, by regiments, and by individuals, officers, soldiers, and by some soldiers' wives. A number of Portuguese men, including some of the dealers, enrolled as muleteers or servants. Their standards varied considerably; some with experience of mules were good, others stupid, using cruelty to drive their mules. A number found campaigning too tough and deserted taking their mules with them. In Portugal the roads were particularly bad, in winter turning into streams of mud. There was always a shortage of mules: Wellington's total of 500 in 1808 had been very seriously inadequate. Few French mules were captured. French commanders, notably Masséna, made a habit of hamstringing their mules during a retreat to prevent their use by the British and to create terror.

The Commissariat and Wellington's headquarters issued a number of instructions concerning the allocation and use of mules. Regiments and battalions received mules according to their muster strength – one mule for six infantry soldiers and two for each four cavalry troopers was the basis for planning and the availability of sufficient animals. Wellington personally believed that pack mules were more efficient than mules pulling the unwieldy local carts but, nevertheless, carts were essential for some roles and were much used, particularly for the sick and wounded. Subaltern lieutenants were allowed one mule for two officers for their personal kit, a captain was allowed one mule or a horse, and more senior officers, were allowed more animals. Many middle-ranking officers bought a horse for journeys and used their mules for baggage with the aid of a local servant boy. These sometimes disappeared with the mule and some of the officers' property. One mule, or much less often a packhorse, was needed for each infantry company or cavalry troop to carry the large cooking kettles. In addition an infantry battalion required five mules and a cavalry regiment six to carry the paymaster's books, surgeons chest and armourer tools and for cavalry regiments the extra mule for a very crude veterinary chest. Wellington's headquarters required eighty mules.

Frequent abuses of the system inevitably occurred. Senior officers would commandeer a mule from any source open to them, including regimental mules. If a regimental mule fell ill or died regimental officers would try and grab a mule open to them, including mules of another regiment despite any regulation from the Commissariat. The use of regimental soldiers as personal batmen was strictly forbidden, but senior officers often required a mule, sometimes two for their personal baggage.

A number of soldiers' wives, four to six in a company of eighty, were permitted to accompany their husbands on a campaign. For the Peninsula they usually purchased a mule or a donkey. On the march they usually followed behind their husband's unit. If a soldier-husband was killed, a quick second marriage usually followed. Bullock-drawn carts in small numbers were used in most operations but their travel speed, two miles an hour at best, was slower than the speed of the mule and the animals required more food. In consequence bullock carts were progressively reduced to the carrying of the wounded and sick, a task also carried out by mules. When fit enough, wounded men would sit astride the mule, who would be guided by a muleteer, but slippery or stony terrain made such travel very painful. More seriously wounded were carried on stretchers improvised from blankets and wooden poles that were carried by two mules tied together.

Every day during the four-year conflict, a long train of pack mules would set out under the charge of Commissariat officers; near the end of the campaign these trains became dignified with the title of Royal Waggon Trains. The line of communication from Lisbon where the food and stores ships arrived could extend up to 400 miles and was unlikely to be able to offer any local resources for purchase. The problem was eased in 1813 when the army took Santander on Spain's north coast. While mules were still in short supply, the growing size of Wellington's army needs, some 9,000 mules for the 53,000 men in 1810, was being met by bringing across mules from North Africa and improved standards of handling by muleteers, who were now on contracts. Fit, experienced young men would jog alongside the mules for four or more hours, remaining cheerful and for the most part honest. They were organised into brigade teams under a respected leader called a *capataz* paid a dollar a day for each mule, plus a dollar or rations for themselves. They were supposed to be fully responsible for their animals but their dollar payments were very often months or more in arrears necessitating a revised arrangement whereby a muleteer was paid only two-thirds of a dollar per day and the Commissariat supplied eight pounds of corn each day for each mule. Most of the *capataz* were reliable and respected but, inevitably, there was occasional friction with British officers or friction between Spaniards and Portuguese. Individuals, *capataz* and units often developed a real affection for their mules, giving them names such as "Queen", "Count" or "Frigate". In France when the fighting ended units held race meetings for horses and mules. Some of the latter required the rider to sit on the mule facing backwards, while a muleteer ran in front of the mule dangling a carrot or hay under its nose. On at least one meeting, a silver cup was awarded to the winning rider. Less fortunate was the adherence of many *capataz* to the Arab custom of not allowing mules to lie down in pens or stables. For day to day basic care farrier sergeants would supervise or personally cleaning and clipping with, at the end of a day's march, hoof or shoeing needs.

Trains would be formed up in five or six component groups with the *capataz* as head driver and mules in files of two or three depending on the terrain. The whole train comprising several scores of mules would extend to six miles, sometimes more in length. Sometimes all mules would carry a light bell, other trains only allowed a bell for the mule of the *capataz*. Journeys were made in several stages with staging posts where loads and teams might change over. As the train neared the combat zone armed military escorts, sometimes from newly arriving drafts or men who had been convalescing at a staging post and were now due to return to their regiments. These men, apparently, were liable to be tempted by the train and would help themselves.

The stores carried by the mules would include food, in the form of ships' biscuits, bread, meat, wine barrels, rum, trusses of hay and forage for the mules, tents and blankets. The strongest mules would carry artillery pieces and ammunition. The tent mules were usually placed to arrive at or near as possible to the front-line regiments. Battalions and regiments own, smaller, packs of mules were required to carry three days' worth of food, water and forage together with blankets and cooking kettles. By the end of 1811 the numbers of mules in use had increased to over 10,000 and a formal daily ration scale for mules instituted – 5lbs of oats, barley or Indian corn and 10lbs of cut straw.

A few final features involving mules and special to this campaign merit mention. Care had to be taken to ensure that mules working with horses were all of the same sex for both animals. On some occasions a single mule would be used by a regimental intelligence officer disguised as a local farmer for what the officer hoped would be a useful reconnaissance. Retreats, when unexpected and urgent could present particular cart problems, moving too hastily and crashing into the cart ahead, or slipping and blocking the way for following carts. The safe and timely arrival of the long mule trains at forward staging post could affect planned operations. If the train was late a planned operation might have to be deferred or several hundred soldiers could be left with little or no food for several days. In the autumn of 1812 one battalion had to wait several weeks before the mule train arrived with the winter clothing. And also any arrival arrangements had to be made for the mules' return journey carrying the sick and wounded but retaining for their own use some of the forage with which they had arrived.

One special problem in a retreat was the custom of placing

wives and any other women camp followers with their mules at the head of a retreating column all at a moment when speed was crucial. In atmospheres of alarm, fear and panic arrangements could become disordered. On a few occasions the mules of women protesting against the retreat had to be shot as a lesson to restore authority and enable the retreat to proceed. Rapid retreats also often meant abandonment and starvation for mules.

When Wellington entered south-west France and advanced further northward, transport problems eased. There were local resources available for requisitioning (often paid for), ports were available to receive supplies from England. Mules were no longer so necessary and numbers were run down. Those remaining were mainly carrying supplies and 6 or 9-pdr gun ammunition for the twelve troops or brigades of the Horse or Field Artillery, with a total of some 1,100 present at Waterloo in June 1815. At Waterloo and after these roles were extended to casualty evacuation.

The Royal Navy had secured Sicily with a British garrison against Napoleon but an attempted invasion of southern Italy in 1806 was a failure. The attempt was ill prepared and inadequate, the invading force withdrew back to Sicily. Mules had been used to transport mountain artillery guns and carry cooking kettles.

After the long war over the Royal Waggon Train's establishment was further reduced and, in 1833, finally abolished. The British Army was not to fight on any western European field again for a hundred years. But in the Peninsula campaign the patient, long-suffering, docile, obedient mule had earned its place in military history and its value was to be seen throughout the far-flung imperial campaigns of the 19th century.

3

The 19ᵗʰ Century: Crimea, India, Ethiopia

The eighty-five years after Waterloo saw Great Britain steadily developing into a lead power in world affairs following its industrial growth. The years saw the nation involved in only major European war, an expansion of empire in Asia based on British rule in India and, of particular interest for this study, a massive development in veterinary knowledge. This chapter will record each of these three facets of the century in turn. All three facets are background for any history of the military mule in British forces.

The Crimean War

The one European theatre conflict, a war in alliance with France against Russia known to history as the Crimean War lasted from 1854 to 1856. The causes of the war still remain much debated but can here be simplified to include, overtly, British public concern over Russian ambitions in Wallachia and Moldavia, with, covertly, concern that these ambitions might extend beyond the Black Sea to Constantinople, so providing Russia with naval opportunities in the eastern Mediterranean to challenge British routes to India. Also present were the ambitions of the French emperor to legitimise his regime by military renown.

The Crimean War will always remain one of the most disastrous examples of a conflict both badly prepared and badly conducted, imposing appalling and unnecessary suffering on soldiers and animals alike.

Clear totals of the British Army mules at work in Crimea are not easy to establish: records and histories refer to "horses and mules". Also a number of mules that had arrived in Anatolia for the campaign could not be transported across the sea because, particularly in the early months, neither the shipping nor forage was available for animals. At this stage the total appears to have been below eighty, with very few carts. This shortage, with also the poor quality of locally recruited muleteers and drivers, led to a necessary move to pack mules rather than two-wheel cart pulling by a single mule. By early 1854 efforts were in hand to transport some 5,000 mules from Italy and Spain to the Crimea; the Spanish mules being preferred and the difficulties of winter rain, snow and mud were better appreciated.

On their arrival, they were distributed out into teams of seven and they were made over to the charge of a *capalay*, who was responsible food, a daily nose-bag of 1¼ quart of Indian corn and, if any was available, grazing. The *capalay's* equipment included farriers' tools. On the march *capalays* would often lead their teams accompanied by a veteran mare with a bell around her neck for mules to follow. The mules' most important loads were poles and cattle hides to make rough and ready tentage for the soldiers. At night the mules would have their harness removed and be allowed to roll; they would then be fastened to rows of poles. Watch against theft had to be maintained.

In the September to October operations, including the

famous battles of the Alma, Balaklava and Inkerman, mules were at work carrying ammunition and supplies and casualties from the battlefields. At least these men could be away from the front line, if only to be given the most rudimentary medical treatment and exposed to little or no shelter against the elements. On at least one occasion mules allocated to an infantry regiment for supply were taken over by the artillery to pull guns, so short was the supply.

Of rather more, and especial, value for the transport of British Army's wounded and sick from the heights surrounding Sevastopol during the fortress-city's long siege, were the mules of the French Army's ambulance corps. Each day many men were evacuated by some of the 500–strong mules that were equipped with either a *cacolet* (a pair of seats), or a pair of litters suspended on either side of a mule's pack saddle. On one day 600 casualties were evacuated by these means. Also in use by the French to help British casualties were *arabas*, four-wheeled carriages without covers or springs pulled by four mules or horses arranged in pairs; these were much in use moving casualties to the Balaklava wharf for embarkation on the voyage to the military hospital at Scutari in Anatolia, which was tended by Florence Nightingale. The French muleteers were generally friendly but not always so. More difficult still were local carriages hired from Crimean Tartars at the rate of Shs. 3/4d per day but where the drivers had to be detained overnight in guarded enclosures to ensure that they would be again available on the following morning.

Sevastopol was finally taken in September 1855 and an armistice signed in February 1856, British troops remaining in the area until 1857. They were supplied by a variety of animals including pack mules in a newly formed Land Transport Corps.

India and Imperial Expansion 1815-1868

The British period in the history of India saw frequent and numerous campaigns and operations to secure British supremacy and the gradual build-up of British authority to rule over, in modern terms India, Pakistan, Bangladesh and Burma. A brief summary of the various operations may be useful, the importance of India and her soldiers in major international and world wars is set out in the special major war chapters that follow.

England's first formal contact with India took place in 1600 when Queen Elizabeth I authorised a Royal Charter to an 'East India Company' that had gathered together a number of small trading companies already in business. Bombay (Mumbai) passed into formal British national sovereignty in 1661 as part of the dowry of Queen Catherine of Braganza on her marriage to Charles II; it was a little later sold to the company (for £10). Chartered company rule was extended over large areas of India in the 18th century, in the course of which French rival imperial ambitions and armies were defeated by forces led by British officers in the company's services. The first British Army regiment to support the company arrived in 1764, many scores more were to follow. Company rule was headed by a British government-appointed Governor-General and three devolved 'Presidencies' – Bombay, Madras and Calcutta – each with its own army with British officers commanding the presidency's regiments. The 1858 'Indian Mutiny' nationalist uprisings, sparked off by mutiny in Bengal Army regiments, showed up all too clearly the obsolescence and weakness of the whole chartered company system and the British government took over paramountcy and full control for India. A little later, in 1877, Queen Victoria was proclaimed "Empress of India" with to follow her successors as "Emperor". The company-era Governor-General was replaced by an imposingly titled "Viceroy". The armies of the three presidencies were combined to form a united Indian Army in the 1880s, which under senior British command and regimental field officers was to last until the end of the Second World War. Independence for the sub-continent created an India with a majority Hindu population and Pakistan with a Muslim majority in August 1947.

"The Army in India" was the term used to define the combination of the King's British Army units – almost entirely infantry, cavalry and artillery – serving alongside the King-Emperor's very much larger Indian Army's infantry and cavalry regiments (but not field artillery until the 1930s), which were commanded and officered by British officers. Indian officers received a 'Viceroy's Commission' though from the end of the First World War a small but steadily increasing number of Indians after training at Sandhurst or a newly created Indian Military Academy received the King's Commission. Also existing within this system were a small number of armies of the major feudatory princes within the Empire of India, discreetly supervised by British officers. The Indian Army played a key role in the entire imperial defence system, most notably in the two World Wars, only coming to an end in 1947. Among the contributions of the Indian Army was its demonstration of the value of the mule in most forms of military operations in India itself and on the wider world stage, though the full value was only fully appreciated in the second half of the century, when the strength, stamina and full potential of the progeny of an indigenous, wild Jack Ass male with a mare had been fully appreciated.

Earlier local campaigns over difficult terrain had provided a lesson, the Commissariats saw that the best possible means of delivering large quantities of supplies was the mule, as it was faster than bullocks, camels or porters and required much less road space. Further, the mule was cost-effective and, with large numbers available in the Punjab, in ample supply. By long tradition, Indian governments had the right to commandeer men and animals, paying a peace-time rate of hire to landlords. It was a system less expensive than the purchase of animals, for the landlord's tenant small holders were drafted to look after their own mules on the march in a campaign. If they refused, they would lose their livelihood. After a campaign was over, mules and muleteers returned to their stockmen and houses and the government was not faced with the costs of large remount depots. This system, which was ideal for small campaigns, proved inadequate when very large numbers of mules were required for large theatres of operations when requisitioning such numbers took time to transport, train and accustom to military life – irregular water and forage, long marches, probable extremes of heat and cold, inexperienced and callous drivers and the noise of battle.

A third and very important factor was to come from the formation of the first two specific mountain batteries in 1851 and 1857; the first battery was equipped with 3-pdr guns, the second with 12-pdr howitzers. Both weapons were smooth bore and muzzle-loading, and they were transported in carriages, to prove very useful as close-support artillery provided the carriages could traverse the ground. British Army mountain mule batteries featured in the 1865 Bhutan campaign, after which British and Indian army batteries were equipped with 7-pdr shell guns to last until 1902.

The lesson was drawn from the campaigns of the first half of the century, which were aimed at the extension of British authority over north and north-west India in which few mules were used other than a small number carrying officers' equipment and personal kit. The first three 19th century campaigns, the 1814–15 Nepal War, the 1817–19 Pindari campaign and the 1824–26 First Burma War all showed up very clearly the unsuitability of camels and bullocks in mountain country, while mules and mountain artillery were emerging as the most important animal asset.

Fig. 1 Mid 19th century Ordnance Mule as used in Mountain Batteries,
muzzle loaded, shell 7lbs, range 3000 yards
(courtesy British Mule Society)

The events of 1857 to 1858, known in British history as the
"Indian Mutiny", formed twenty months of military operations
and heavy fighting but again do not seem to have included
mules in any great number, even in transport. The British
and French intervention in China, in which the Taku forts
and Beijing were taken, involved mules among the transport
trains but the operation took longer than it should have done.
Local Chinese subverted the Chinese muleteers of the advance
column, departing with their mules during one confused
night. Another setback followed in the 1863 northern Punjab
campaign suppressing Hindu nationalist insurgents. Bad,
hurried planning led to the selection for the first phase of
a route for the military force so overhung with rocks and
boulders as to be impassable, knocking loads off the backs of
the mules in total confusion.

In 1867–68 there followed Ethiopia, the most striking of

the century's imperial campaigns, one in which large numbers of mules were to play a lead role, the expedition into Abyssinia (now Ethiopia), a campaign proving beyond all doubt that the pack mule was the best provider for supply to a large field force fighting in mountains.

Ethiopia in the mid-19th century was in a period of anarchy with ongoing fighting between regional warlord princes. From this fighting one prince, Kassa Hailu, emerged as the winner, proclaiming himself Emperor Tewodros II. As emperor he developed grandiose ambitions for his country and himself, among them the acquisition of modern military weaponry, including 12 and 15-inch mortars for his army with for himself a megalomaniac claim to be the ruler of other kings and of half the world. His half-crazed rule became increasingly cruel and bloodthirsty, to be fiercely opposed by the other regional warlords. His violence turned on to British citizens living at the time in Ethiopia after the Foreign Office in London had unwisely neglected to reply to a letter he had written to Queen Victoria. The British Consul at Gondar was arrested and thrown into prison; other Britons, including wives and children, were also thrown into prison. Tewodros himself prepared a mountain bastion retreat at Magdala in what is now Wollo province, the centre of the northern highlands of Ethiopia.

Great Britain in the mid-1860s was at the height of imperial power and not prepared to accept such treatment. A relief force was assembled by the Bombay presidency government in India in 1867 and shipped across to a small Red Sea port, Zula, in a bay south of Massawa, at the time known as Annesley Bay. The force was composed of four Indian Army cavalry and ten Indian infantry regiments, two, later three, British Army infantry battalions, a squadron of British cavalry, horse and mortar artillery batteries, a Royal Navy rocket troop and a 3,000 strong Indian labour force – a total of 12,000 men. It was commanded by General Sir Robert Napier, who arrived at Zula on 7th January, 1868.

For transport and supply an initial forty-two elephants, 5,108 mules and ponies, 1,839 camels, 962 bullocks and 286 bullock carts had been landed together with six million pounds of fodder and five million pounds of provisions and a further 13,000 mules had been purchased to follow. The elephants and camels were thought necessary, the weight and size being thought too heavy for mules accustomed to the smaller guns in use in India. The additional mules were recruited from as far away as Syria. The administrative arrangements at Zula were, however, chaotic, as the warm clothing needed for the mountain region had not arrived. Unskilled muleteers failed to understand the mule pack harness; the animals themselves were wandering around the port area in search of food and water. The first muleteers recruited were ill-disciplined and wantonly cruel; these had to be replaced quickly by 5,000 Punjabis but a number of strayed and starving mules died. Others more fortunate were taken over by soldiers from the two British battalions and well cared for. For the force as a whole a special order was issued requiring one soldier or muleteer for each animal. For the first time in British Army history "sick depots" for animals were established along the line of advance. These depots were crude and the staff poorly trained but they were of some value. From the early days of the march mules were stricken with glanders, with numbers dying.

Napier quickly restored a firm command and prepared his operational plan for the 400–mile march to Magdala. Before his arrival, advance parties had recommended and prepared a route for the first stage. The main body was grouped into two brigades each with one of the British battalions followed – the third British battalion had been delayed at sea. A light railway had been laid out for the first stage but further inland became

Fig. 2 The Abyssinian Expedition: Return of the Army From Magdala – The Mountain Train, 1868 (courtesy Mary Evans Picture Library)

a succession of tableland plateaux described succinctly by one soldier: "If this was a table and the table had been turned upside down and the troops had to climb all four legs". It was found that the best service from the mules was by firmly dragging rather than driving them on with the whip.

Tewodros had burnt down villages and small community settlements in his retreat inland and the day's marches were continually harassed by men principally aiming to capture mules. Scorching heat and water shortages added to the difficulties of soldiers and animals. Worse was to follow when the columns entered the mountain areas, with very narrow paths on the steep slopes of deep gorges – the latter were liable to torrential flooding after heavy rainfall. Further into the mountains slopes became crag-sided, in many cases sheer, vertical and precipitous, narrow crevices providing the only pathways. In the narrowest pathways soldiers went ahead of the mules to try and widen the tracks. Nights became bitterly cold for which the issue uniforms were totally inadequate. The mule supply system had to be just the bare essentials, food, water, tentage and forage for the animals. The normal battalion establishment of 1,000 mules and 600 muleteers was, for the final assault, reduced to 187 mules and sixty-nine muleteers with loads reduced from 150 to 100lbs.

As the regiments approached Magdala, Tewodros surrendered the British hostages and then, later on 10th April he committed suicide after losing a brief battle. His stronghold, a bastion approximately 1,200 feet above a 9,000 feet high plateau table, was stormed shortly afterwards. The force then began the return journey back to Zula, which was only slightly less hazardous. No figure for the death-rate of mules survives. The numbers would have been considerable, though one Indian cavalry regiment was tasked specifically to escort sick mules.

While other larger animals had carried the decisive

weaponry, the mules had carried supplies, in particular water without which the campaign could not have been fought. Several thousand more mules had arrived at Zula during the campaign, making a total at the time of 12,000 mules at work with a further 6,000 ordered who arrived in the final stages or too late. In the transport train's arrangements there were 400 Indian and 160 European inspectors and eighty commissioned officers at work with animals. The Ethiopia campaign was a major landmark in the history of the military mule.

The slow move of military opinion towards the mule in supply service was indicated in 1860 when for the first time pack mules had been introduced in government transport. Within the military 1,000 mules replaced camels in Rawalpindi and Peshawar. In 1865 an improved 7-pdr gun was introduced for mountain battery contingents. By the late 1870s the change in military thinking was showing clear results. In the 1877–79 fighting in South Africa, in Natal and the Zulu War, over 800 mules were brought in from Spain, Italy and Austria, and a further 2,000 purchased locally. In the badly managed Second Afghan War of 1878–81 many thousands of camels died because of poor or total absence of forage. Three Mountain Batteries, two British and one Indian, over 450 mules were taken by General Roberts on his famous march from Kabul to Kandahar. In Egypt in 1882 in operations to suppress the uprising of Colonel Arabi, the Indian Army division included a full complement of 4,816 mules and the final total involved was over a thousand. Four years later in the Sudan operation to secure the port of Suakin over 2,000 mules were at work mostly in water cart supply; they suffered a number of casualties. In the same year, 1883, 637 mules provided supplies for a punitive expedition in Bechuanaland, South Africa. Back in India in 1887 the two brigade force used to suppress the Mohmand uprising included 1,628 mules. In 1889–90 2,237 mules served in the force sent to assert imperial authority at Chittagong on the east coast of the

Bay of Bengal. In the 1890 Zhob Valley operation in North India four mule Mountain Batteries served in the force. In two further North India operations, the 1895 Chitral Himalayan Expedition and the 1897–98 Tochi Field Force in Waziristan 8,210 and 4,290 mules served in the columns. In the 1892–98 Tirah Field Force employed over 10,000 mules of which 912 went on to be part of the follow-up Bunerwal Force to reassert imperial authority. The securing of stability in the British controlled region of Somaliland at the turn of the century required the support of 200 mules; further numbers were needed in 1912–14. Colonel Younghusband's famous 1903–04 expedition into Tibet included 7,096 mules, 910 becoming casualties. A British Mountain Battery was included in the force; it fired its guns from the top of a 17,200–foot ridge.

Two further, more general developments in warfare and the actual conduct of war in the 19th century are of importance: the first concerned signal communication, the second supply procedure arrangements.

From the time of the Crimean War the Army had been developing field communications, from the very basic messenger on horseback to division-level heliograph sections of an officer, six men and three mules for the signallers. The Heliograph equipment and supplies were introduced in the late 1870s. The Second Afghan War saw for the first time the introduction of a field and line train in which a section of three mules now carried six miles of cable, supported by a section of carts pulled by other animals which carried a further twenty miles of cable. A third section carried base line wire and poles for the line telegraph. In the Egypt 1882 expedition a cable section that had been carried by mules proved very valuable, and further cable sections continued the development of cable communication in India until the First World War. In Britain experiments were conducted by the Royal Engineers, though horses rather than mules were used for transport.

Fig. 3 Mules carrying poles for signals. Half a mile of poles
could be carried in three containers (Courtesy Royal Signals)

The second development, in 1898 sought to provide long-
overdue and much needed regulations clarifying responsibilities
for the arrangements for supply from bases, parks and depots
some way behind the forward edges of battle to the actual
front line. First line transport for battle would be the duties of
a regiment and its personnel, and include ammunition, stores,
signalling equipment, trench equipment, water carts and a little
later casualty evacuation. Each unit, regiment or battalion would
have an officer and staff for these duties when these materials
essential for combat reached a regiment's rear area lines.
Second line equipment, essential for subsistence – blankets,
tentage, rations and forage for one day or more – would be the
responsibilities of Army supply staff for outloading at agreed
suitable sites. Mules figured in both, more often in the second

line transport, though frequently having to move into first line duties, especially if a unit had suffered heavy human and animal casualties. In practice and in some theatres the distinction between first and second line often became blurred or ceased to exist, as will be seen in the chapters that follow.

The South African War events appear in the next chapter, but any chapter of events prior to the outbreak of the First World War must include mention of events far removed from India: Antarctica. During his 1911 South Pole Expedition, Captain Scott decided that mules would have been of more use to him than the ponies that he had with him and he asked for Indian mules. Unfortunately these did not reach him in time but were put to use by the search party. In the ice and snow the mules were able to pull the sledges up to fourteen miles a day. At the end of the search, covering 350 miles, two mules died and five were withdrawn only to be shot later.

By August 1914 the total number of military mules maintained by the government of India had reached 28,949, the large majority being in field corps with others in cadres prepared for expansion if necessary. Provision was also made for a supply of mules to support military medical services. Two new versions of the mountain battery screw gun, both breech-loaded and firing a 10lb shell had been developed, the first in 1902 and the second, an improved version, in 1914.

The sequence of events in India, Africa and China show that in the second half of the century the mule was playing a key role in the logistic and artillery support in power projection within and beyond imperial frontiers.

Veterinary Services and Administration

Conditions for animals improved only very slightly at the end of the Napoleonic Wars. A set of regulations for the transport by sea of horses, and probably by extension mules, recommended that in bad weather the faces and noses of animals be washed with vinegar and water, ventilation of the holds of ships be implemented by the ship's sails, the stall on either side of a sick animal was to be left unoccupied, slings were to be used for the loading and unloading of sick animals, and that in hot weather animals be embarked at night after feeding. Nevertheless, sail being long preferred to steam, ships' voyages could often take up to a month and at this time one transport ship was lost at sea following a fire. In the Crimean War there had been some improvement in care, some sick or injured animals were taken to an animal hospital near Varna in Bulgaria, but these had first to be packed into lighters at Balaklava before being hoisted onto a transport ship.

In Britain academic veterinary training developed quickly, leading to a diploma award – farrier training had improved earlier. In 1815 Army Veterinary Department officers were ranked as cornets (the rank of a cavalry subaltern) and accepted as members of officers' messes, though they were forbidden to take military decisions and their further advancement was limited to captaincy. In India an attempt was made to recruit Indian pharmacists and medical orderlies to serve as veterinary officers in the three presidential armies. The project proved a failure and veterinary surgeons were recruited in England; an establishment of thirty-one officers was allowed in the 1800s.

At the outbreak of the Crimean War eighteen out of the Army's strength of forty-five officers was sent out to Crimea. Two years later, in June 1856, the totals were fifty-three out of a strength of sixty-four, and included a 'Principal Veterinary Surgeon' in the Land Transport Corps. Such depots were in the description of the historian of the Royal Army Veterinary Corps: "Unorganised, staffed by untrained veterinary officers, each doing his best in the absence of military knowledge with the limited appliances at hand and the particularly villainous local labour engaged".

British Army organisation remained very poor throughout the century, a frequent cause being the supercilious attitude of cavalry regimental officers to veterinary officers, opposing both funding and status at every level in the Army. In the First 1839–1842 Afghan War, veterinary services were left to regiments, in the Second, 1878–1880, although two base hospitals were established these were understaffed and such staff as was available poorly qualified – 30,000 "baggage animals" died. A small army veterinary school was opened in 1880 and in the following year the cavalry regimental arrangement system finally ended. Of great importance and help to farriers, machine manufacturing of shoes began. This in time led to a change in the attitude of many farriers who, under the terms of the contract system under which they worked at the time, had converted many, in the words of the Veterinary Corps history, into "growling, sulky laggards".

In 1898, the year before the opening of the South Africa War, drastic changes were made in the Army's veterinary services. These were placed in a subordinate position within the Remount Department. Again in the words of the Veterinary Corps historian this change led to "an army being riddled by contagions and deprived of all means of dealing with them. Never in the history of any British War has there been such a deliberate sacrifice of animal life and public money".

No Army veterinary surgeons were consulted before this change. All that was left was a senior officer with no veterinary staff officers at all, though in India an Army Mule College was created. Among the courses provided was one for newly-arrived British officers. One student officer who attended in 1910 was a Lieutenant B.L. Montgomery.

A good deal of experience in basic field veterinary work had, however, been picked up by the end of the century as a result of the numerous 19th century campaigns. In Britain veterinary studies as a university discipline advanced to high quality degrees as a full professional qualification; at a lower level, farrier training was again improved and regularised. One factor, though, that was still for some time to limit progress was that so much of military thinking was dominated by cavalry officers and the horse. In the 241 pages of the Veterinary Corps history, veterinary services are presented in the context of horses. Dogs receive one full paragraph while mules appear only *en passant* in one sentence in one paragraph in the entire work concerned with 19th century campaigning.

4

The War in South Africa 1898-1902

In the years 1899–1902 South Africa was to be the scene of a bitter and bloody conflict essentially between the two white communities in the country: the Afrikaner people in the land-locked provinces of the Orange Free State and the Transvaal against the British government support for the English-speaking peoples of Cape Colony and Natal, both with access to the sea. Involvement of the Indians in Natal, the non-white peoples of the Cape and indigenous African peoples was considerable and unhappy. The two Afrikaner provinces had in 1998 a limited internal self-government under an overall somewhat vague British suzerainty, but they retained a strong dislike, amounting to a hatred, of the British and the British community dating from the Great Trek in the 1830s. In the 1890s clashes and conflicts of interest – economic after the discovery of gold in the Transvaal and social in the challenge to the traditional Afrikaner way of life and the Afrikaans language had risen from the influx of British and other European peoples. On 11th October 1899 the two Afrikaner governments declared war and the South African high veldt became a vast battlefield.

The many international, imperial and other factors around the war must lie outside this work, but one directly affecting mules was that the war was to be the last in all sectors and operations that was totally dependent throughout on animal transport for supply. In the fighting horses and draught oxen all played lead roles but large numbers of mules were involved – and generally treated worse than the others. It was also the first war in which the machine gun, often carried by mules, and the 7-pdr rifle-barrelled, muzzle-loaded screw-gun appeared outside India.

Despite all the clear indications that conflict was inevitable, Britain was very poorly prepared for warfare in South Africa. Despite the long distances that were likely to be the terrain in a war with the two Boer states there were only 12,000 mules to hand in South Africa in October 1899; by the end of the campaign, the total had reached some 120,000. Over 100,000 mules were imported from India, Great Britain, the United States, Italy, Ceylon, Mauritius and Cyprus. The 90,000 American mules generally cost between £12 and £15, the larger Missouri mules up to £25. The 7,000 Italian mules cost between £20 and £32, the 15,000 from Spain £20 each.

The importing was generally arranged in ships not fitted with stalls. The mules had to endure severe suffering and fear in rough weather while tightly packed together in ships' holds, with 2,816 dying of suffocation or being killed while at sea. The 1898 War Office reductions had meant that there were no military veterinary services at all in South Africa at the start of the war. Field veterinary services had to be requested from India before field sections and field veterinary hospital staff could arrive from Britain, and even then veterinary services, especially for mules, remained very poor throughout the war. Fortunately the soft ground of the veldt meant the mules did not require shoes and the tens of thousands of shoes sent out from Britain were hardly ever used. The inexperience of muleteers had led to a mule stampede two days before the war began, over forty mules being lost.

The Boers had opened the fighting immediately with an

advance into Natal and were soon besieging Mafeking, Kimberley and Ladysmith. In the sieges military and civilians suffered alike; at Mafeking minted roast mule with curried locusts was on menus for the garrison. A series of reverses for the British Army lasted until January 1890 when more competent British authority followed the arrival of Britain's two leading soldiers: Generals Roberts and Kitchener. One of the first actions of Roberts as early as January 1890 was to issue very firm instructions, to be read out to all concerned, for the immediate ending of the brutal mishandling of mules by muleteers, the uncontrolled whipping and cruelty that had been left uncontrolled. Especially cruel personnel were punished. Later, in June 1900 Roberts set up a scheme whereby drivers of support companies with or including mules received a cash award of £5 for taking good care of their mules. At least one novel idea for regimental commanders directed that when time permitted packs should be removed from mules to give a period of release but many commanders remained in the words of one historian "scandalously careless in the matter of working their mules to death".

Roberts and Kitchener reorganised the whole administration and supply transport as well as the fighting command. Two mule companies each of 520 mules and fifty-one wagons or carts could keep an infantry division or a cavalry brigade supplied with food, forage and necessary baggage for two days. With the shortage of mules, however, meeting the requirement that both regimental and general supply store columns be mule driven was to lead to some reductions in the number of mules available for medical services. Numbers of mules were also needed for water carts. Mules were the main but not the only animal used in telegraph communication line work, the terrain requiring mules for equipment draught carriage work. Some 18,000 miles of ground line were laid and 9,360 miles of poles and line erected. Early attempts at the use of wireless proved a failure.

Despite resolute resistance the sheer numbers of British troops began to turn the tide against the Boers. The sieges of Kimberley and Ladysmith were ended in February, Mafeking after seven months in March, and the Orange River Colony was cleared of Boer military at the end of the same month. Invasion of the Transvaal followed in May with 58,000 mules in support; the occupation of Pretoria in July ended formal resistance, the final entry combat advance was supported by 22,000 mules. British forces, by then reaching a total of some 500,000 men, had nevertheless to face a Boer guerrilla campaign, which challenge they met with the herding of Boer women and children into concentration camps where many died. A formal peace treaty was concluded on 31st May 1902.

Mules had played a vital part in transport throughout the war. Oxen were found to have limitations: their inability to endure heat and liability to fall ill from disease. The pace at which they moved and their need of daylight for grazing limited the roles for which they could be used. Mules, although carrying a slightly lighter load, could move more quickly and consume forage at any time of day or night if grazing was not available. Mule train columns although longer could travel faster and over greater daily distances, a factor of importance on the high veldt, but also over the whole three years of the war 51,399 mules had been killed, had died or were destroyed. A veterinary historian commented that the "endurance of spirit and willingness of the mule was the admiration of the Army", concluding particularly in respect of the smaller mules "nothing in the way of an animal approaches the small mule for true grit". Especially appreciative were the Royal Artillery where despite much indignation when mules were first posted to the batteries an artillery historian was able to write of one Royal Horst Artillery battery commander who personally directed the battery's guns while seated on a cream coloured mule.

5

The First World War 1914–1918

The shortcomings and failures of the British Army in South Africa led to significant military reforms. Among these were improvements in medical and veterinary services, the latter arguably much more concerned with horses rather than mules but in theory applicable to both. Following recommendations of a parliamentary committee an Army Veterinary Corps, A.V.C., was established in 1903. Its Director-General was a full colonel but he was entitled "to rank as a Major-General". Four veterinary hospitals and field veterinary sections were created for active operations, all to be staffed by trained personnel. By 1910 the strength of the A.V.C. was 368, of which 160 were officers. The newly created Territorial Force included a reserve of 148 professional veterinary officers. After the end of the First World War on 27th November 1918, King George V authorised the title of Royal Army Veterinary Corps.

The role of mules in the war, including A.V.C. veterinary support is best set out in sections of this chapter for each theatre, but reference should be made here to the growing professionalism, experience and concern for the welfare of all animals which developed greatly during the war.

At the outbreak of war, Great Britain had no mules on its

strength in the British Isles, the Indian Army had about 6,000, of which over half were with the mountain regiments. During the four years of the war mules arrived for the different theatres from the United States, Argentina, Uruguay, Spain, Portugal, Canada, India, Egypt, Greece and Cyprus, many not broken in. Most had long and unpleasant sea and rail journeys. The new regulations for animals carried by British vessels would have made the sea journeys less hard on those ships where they were applied, but conditions on vessels under other flags and even on British ships at times of urgent movement needs were often far from satisfactory. Even in the better vessels mules might be marched, sometimes pulled, dragged or pushed along a gangway plank, often temporarily blinded. Several transport ships were sunk by German submarines; on one occasion, when a transport ran aground at Halifax, Nova Scotia 101 mules managed to swim ashore, only two being drowned. Also, as the war progressed, shipping space for forage came to be questioned at a time when petrol engine motor transport was becoming available with, for men, a motor mechanic career appearing more attractive than that of a muleteer. Fewer and fewer became available to prepare a well-balanced mule pack or harness. But 75 per cent of the rounds of ammunition fired in the first three years of the war had been carried by mules; over 219,000 mules were still on active service and over the full four years of the war between three and 400,000 mules were estimated to have served in one theatre or another. By November 1918, 25,097 mules had been shipped from North America, 1,500 from South America and 3,700 from Spain and Portugal for use in different theatres of the war.

The Western Front 1914–18

The services of mules on the Western Front needs greater recognition than it has received, perhaps not only due to the tremendous scale of the fighting, human casualties and suffering but also regrettably due to an element of prejudice. In the thirty-five pages of the *Official Veterinary History*, devoted to the Western Front there is full material on horses, occasional references to "other animals", but the word mule hardly ever appears. In fact in the first months of the war when there was no other transport mules played a vital part in operations from as early as October 1914 in the First Battle of Ypres following the arrival, in stages, of 8,000 mules from the Indian Army Transport Corps. They were divided into eleven field corps; each corps possessed nine troops and each troop was commanded by an Indian Army sergeant *daffadar,* or a British warrant officer. The mules of these corps were in the most part from Argentina or Punjabi mules, the offspring of donkeys and pony mares. Their roles, to last for the next three years was a mix of field gun pulling, draught cart pulling for engineering equipment, ammunition, water, rations, entrenching spades and shovels, barbed wire or packs of smaller items of equipment. Much was delivered in carts pulled by two mules and delivered to rear collecting points for onward transport by regiments whose pack mules would take rations and ammunition up to front-line trenches.

Numbers steadily increased despite the arrival of motor transport from 1916 onwards. On 31st August 1918 there were 81,060 British Army mules at work on the Western Front in France, mostly now light draught or pack serving the British Expeditionary Force of over forty divisions. Totals will have varied at different times as in 1917–18 divisions were moved to the Middle East, Macedonia or Italy. On arrival in the different theatres they were graded into classes, heavy loads, artillery cart pullers, cart pullers with especial roles and basic back pack.

While many mules were working safely in transport out of range of German guns, mule casualties among those at the front from bombing, shelling and gas were massive: 5,480 killed, of which 178 were from gas attacks and 69,400 wounded in battles over the years of trench warfare. It was found possible to protect many mules against chlorine gas but there was no protection for them against mustard gas. Many others were injured by the German practice before a withdrawal of scattering spikes, known as caltrops, that landed on soft mud tracks and paths doing serious damage to mules' hooves. Also, unfortunately, many mules frustrated by the confines of trenches would kick each other causing injury, sometimes serious. Score of mules towed field and medium artillery guns and carried supplies and ammunition forward where roads no longer existed in the conditions of evil-smelling mud, slime and slippery paths, debris and shell craters with shells and flares bursting around them and the tracks to the gun positions littered by the corpses of mules and horses. A number carrying heavy loads sank too deeply into mud to be extricated and had to be destroyed with a shot; others died from sheer exhaustion. On many occasions teams of mules would be tasked with pulling carts, motor vehicles and even tanks out of the mud. Forage and shelter were generally inadequate and often non-existent. Mule fortitude, patience and stamina was severely tested and widely admired but overwork, exhaustion and debility was the result for many.

As the newly raised "Kitchener Army" battalions arrived in France mule transport was attached to each unit. In many battalions the mules soon became respected and well liked. When not in the line in rest periods regiments would include mules in unit and inter-unit sports, including mule races bare-back, officer, sergeant and soldier inter-company races and jumping. As late as July 1918 in the Second Battle of the Marne, fought in very difficult terrain, mules were still engaged in their vital roles of ammunition supply and casualty evacuation. The experience of the previous fifty years was put to use with the wounded and sick. Cacolets for wounded capable of sitting upright or lying on stretchers on each side of the mule were supplemented by travoys, improvised stretchers of poles and blankets placed on the back of a mule or pulled along behind. Both cacolets and travoys appeared on all battlefields.

Fig. 4 The Western Front, August 1917
(courtesy Mary Evans Picture Library)

Fig. 5 Casualty evacuation, Salonika Campaign: Cacolet
(courtesy IWM)

Fig. 6 Casualty evacuation, Salonika Campaign: Travoy
(courtesy IWM)

The Army's veterinary services expanded as more and more British divisions were formed and sent to the front. Initially in 1914 there were six veterinary hospitals, eleven mobile veterinary sections and two base veterinary stores depots. By 1918 this had risen to eighteen 2,000 animal patient hospitals, four convalescent depots each for 1,200 patients, sixteen veterinary evacuation stations and fifty mobile veterinary services, but the standards of training of personnel before their arrival in France varied considerably. The Army's veterinary services were supported and joined by the Royal Society for the Prevention of Cruelty to Animals, which provided four veterinary hospitals, staffing and ambulances. Other animal welfare groups also offered help, providing staff for depots and ambulances. The corpses of some of the mules that died in hospitals were sent back to Britain, the hides forwarded on to tanners and the flesh used to supplement the food for the population in the 1917–18 winter food shortage.

In 1917 and 1918 the British Army was required to provide considerable help to the arriving United States Army. For domestic political reasons the American army at the time had no artillery, aircraft or motor transport. Despite the gallantry shown by American soldiers, from the start the American command had to turn to the French and the British for help. From holdings in Britain over 6,000 mules were supplied to the Americans, many of the animals had in fact been purchased earlier from the United States. Having no military veterinary organisation the Americans were given the use of the British Army veterinary hospitals and horse convalescent depots.

German East Africa 1914–1918

The only other British Army land campaign to last the entire period of the war was that against the Germans in East Africa.

The German East Africa colony comprised territories that are now mainland Tanzania (and not Zanzibar), Rwanda and Burundi, with Dar-es-Salaam as its capital. Within the territory over which much of the campaign was to be fought, mainland Tanzania, a wide tsetse fly belt stretched some 250 miles inland from the coast. Until March 1916 large-scale use of animals was limited to relatively tsetse-free areas; this restriction was then abandoned resulting in the words of the *Official History* "... and ultimate dead wastage of all animals in the force".

The German force comprised well-led, locally recruited African units, military garrison personnel and officers, sailors and some guns and equipment from a German warship. The force was extremely well commanded by General Paul von Lettow-Vorbeck. The British forces at the outset were built upon colonial African regiments together with one metropolitan British infantry battalion, these were later joined by South African regiments and West and Central African colonial battalions. The force was led by incompetent British generals until 1916 when General Jan Smuts of South Africa took command and was later succeeded by a second very competent South African field of battle general, van Deventer.

The campaign opened on the border between the British East Africa Protectorate, now Kenya, and the German colony. In the course of four years the British forces, eventually totalling 130,000 pushed the Germans south into Portuguese Mozambique and then on into Northern Rhodesia, now Zambia. The Germans used their much smaller 4,000 strong force with very great skill. Much of the terrain was bush and scrub, the local inhabitants struggling to survive on a very limited diet and the only local resources available for the forces of either side being the shooting of wild animals. Supply took two forms: load-carrying porters recruited in the East Africa Protectorate and pack mules, commanded with a general callous indifference to the lives of either. No precise figures for carrier porter deaths exist but reliable estimates say some 40,000 men from Kenya died from poor food, overwork, disease and neglect. Porters from other territories, particularly Uganda were treated better but nevertheless many scores of men died.

Some mules were drafted from enterprises of various kinds in Kenya and Uganda, others were imported from South Africa and a number from Ethiopia. These latter were generally small animals, four to four and a half feet high but particularly well-adjusted to rough terrain and resistant to disease and also move more speedily on the march than other breeds, able to carry a soldier with full equipment at four miles per hour over long periods. Forty mules were allotted to each company of a battalion. Official records note some 33,000 mules and 30,000 donkeys were drafted for the campaign. At the Armistice survivors totalled only 897 mules and 1,402 donkeys. Small numbers, eighty mules and 329 donkeys are recorded as having been sold off earlier.

For mules the campaign was one of overwork, irregular feeding and poor care; rations were delayed and in the first two years especially it was not possible to provide grain for the animals of the forward units. In the few grasslands there were many poisonous plants which caused illnesses. Larger wild animals, especially those very much larger and of frightening appearance were terrifying for mules. As one officer wrote later, "Imagine the feelings of a mule which had never before seen in its life anything larger than an Abbottabad bullock, waking up to find an enormous hippo eating his hay". Worst of all was the attitude of many formation and unit commanders, that essential animal personnel such as shoeing smiths were not necessary and should be left behind.

The most serious disease affecting mules was trypanosomiasis in the tsetse belt areas, horse-sickness and a number of small but serious cases of rinderpest. The German military used tactical skills to force the British colonial regiments into terrain of particular tsetse risk. Marches at night hardly, if at all, reduced tsetse attacks, these for some reason often concentrating on the rearguard of advancing units including transport and casualty mules. Some limited effect in treating mules with trypanosomiasis was found with the use of small doses of arsenic, 5g later increased to 10g.

In theory a useful sized veterinary service existed. Regimental staff provided for a veterinary officer, a sergeant, two sergeants and a shoeing smith but these were not always forward with their regiments. Personnel from the different Corps, East African, South African and British officers and non-commissioned officers were frequent victims of malaria and dysentery. A number of veterinary hospitals and mobile veterinary sections were formed but all were also behind the forward battle area. The average life of the front-line mule was about six weeks, if not earlier from being struck by disease caused by overwork exhaustion following a severe reduction in rations.

Behind all the mismanagement and neglect of both porters and animals lay a racially-based indifference. Units of labour, black humans or lowly mules did not greatly matter and were expendable. The author of the *Official Veterinary History* was later to write, "There is no parallel instance for such a colossal waste of animals in any campaign".

Gallipoli 1915

The aim of the 1915 Gallipoli campaign was to open up the Dardanelle sea route and thereby enable warships and troops to occupy, or at least overawe the Ottoman Empire government, with fortune eliminating the Ottoman Turks from the war, opening a flank attack on the Central Powers and provide Russia with support through the Black Sea.

After the failure of a naval attack amphibious assault, landings were made on the Gallipoli peninsula on 25th April 1915: one by British troops landing on the beaches of the extreme South-West Cape Helles area of the peninsula; one landing by Australian and New Zealand troops further up the coast on an area to be known later as Anzac Cove; and a third, diversionary attack by French troops, mostly West African, on the south-east side of the peninsula. This attack was withdrawn later.

The coast of the peninsula was a logistician's nightmare. There were no port or harbour facilities. The first landings had to be made over beaches and some in coves, with only a very narrow beach front and with everywhere steep sloping craggy hills that lay almost immediately inland. As well as the terrain difficulties, others included the need to supply water brought from Egypt, fierce heat in the summer months, cold in the autumn and winter, all together with determined German-led Turkish soldier resistance. In consequence the campaign almost at once became one of deadlock, heavy casualties and severe hardship for soldiers and animals.

In an attempt to break the deadlock a further landing up the coast was made on 15th August at Suvla Bay, where a large bay and a more gently rolling hinterland offered easier ground, but at the landing opposition was stiff. Sixty mules were killed and 133 wounded in the first six days and, over the rest of the campaign, over 2,000 mules were killed at Suvla. The bay provided facilities for lighters and makeshift piers but soldiers could make little or no progress against the now very efficiently organised resistance. As autumn and then winter approached it was decided to end the whole Gallipoli operation and withdraw the force in December.

Pack mules formed the most important part of supply transport throughout the campaign although this was not at first grasped and numbers were inadequate. Mules were brought to the peninsula from Egypt and India, the best being those from the Indian Army mountain batteries. Mules were unloaded from ships onto lighters in slings, or directly onto a makeshift quayside. Some had to swim a last stage. A number were taken from a captured German vessel. Unloading could be chaotic, as the animals were very frightened. Some were blinded, though a fortunate few landed with the food boats. At the campaign's peak, just after the Suvla landings, there were 1,350 mules at Cape Helles, 1,889 at Anzac and after some days at least 2,103 at Suvla. Others were being made ready at Alexandria or on Greek islands. In addition there were thirty small donkeys. These, and the smaller mules were of particular use as they could enter and move around in the trenches carrying water supplies, and also take an injured man in and out of a surgical operating tent. At Suvla a light railway line was laid, mules providing the railway engine power. In their basic duty of the provision of ammunition, water and food to the front line the mules' ability to negotiate small paths in craggy cliffsides and steep hills made them indispensable. Mules might have to be dragged up a cliff side or on the way back pushed along down by sweating, swearing soldiers. Supplies for forward edge of battle trenches had to be delivered under cover of darkness or early morning, otherwise the dust clouds created by mules' movements could make them a target for enemy snipers and artillery. Other duties included casualty evacuation, on occasions transporting a soldier to bring comfort to a dying man. During the evacuation mules were sent forward with empty boxes to be filled with stores for their return march back to the beaches. Under fire terrified mules might scream out, especially if they had been wounded. In the last months of the campaign it was noticed that many mules were overworked and stressed, particularly at times of extreme heat or cold if water or forage was delayed.

For feeding and watering mules would often be lined up on beaches; water was slow in arriving and protest whinnying would follow. Mules, too, were often sensitive to the purity or otherwise of any local water resources. Forage might include oats, barley and maize, sometimes in compressed form. Hay presented a problem, often having to be provided on nets to prevent the wind blowing it all away. It was often not possible to provide the correct balance of food. An additional hazard was one that if hay was eaten straight from the ground it would become mixed with sand and give mules a form of colic; shortages of hay nets added to this risk. At Suvla mules were provided with nosebags.

The muleteers and drivers were often soldiers and volunteers with a liking for animals. Besides the mountain battery mules, others outstanding were 1,500 men from Indian Army transport Mule Corps who had been brought over from France, and a strange 750 mule-strong body of Russian-Jewish exiles called the Zion Mule Corps.

A number of mules were killed in action: between 25th April and 15th August, 200 were killed and 599 wounded. Fifty-four were drowned when the transport lighters carrying them capsized and 129 were killed or wounded in an air raid on Kefalonia on their way to Gallipoli.

Within the limits of the possible efforts were made to provide veterinary care. A veterinary hospital for horses, donkeys and mules was set up at Cape Helles and mobile veterinary sections, in effect small hospitals, on all three areas. Others were at work at the Gallipoli force bases on the islands of Mudros and Imbros and further away in Alexandria. Sick mules were mounted on slings for transport. After treatment many mules that had been injured or sick were able to return to work, but 250 who were so seriously injured or wounded and not thought likely to survive any form of transport, even a sling, were shot.

Carcases of dead mules were to create another problem in the confined spaces of the beachheads. Burial digging seemed, and was, too heavy a burden to place upon soldiers already exhausted and dispirited. Some carcases were washed out to sea, while others were filled with stones and towed out to sea. Apparently the carcases would turn upside down and on at least one occasion a mule's leg sticking out of the water was mistaken for the periscope of an enemy submarine.

The December 1915 evacuation was outstandingly well prepared and organised, with 3,752 mules and forty-four donkeys being successfully embarked, but 200 mules and forty donkeys were recorded as killed or missing.

Gallipoli remains a British, Australian and New Zealand military epic. Estimates of British and Dominion casualties vary, but a little over 200,000 is near the truth. There can be no doubt that had it not been for the services of mules in casualty evacuation, stores and water supply the total would have been very much higher.

The Balkans 1915–1918

The campaign, beginning in Greece but which by the end of the war had extended into Macedonia and Serbia involved six British Army divisions. It was French-inspired and remained throughout its three years under French supreme command, not always followed by the British. Its overt aim, to try to defend or later liberate Serbia, was admirable, but behind this lay French domestic political in-fighting and French aims for the region in the post-war world. The first British divisions arrived in the theatre without any transport, a situation not helped by the unwilling attitude of many Greeks, whose country was technically neutral until June 1917, to help with mule or horse transport. The Balkan terrain inland was mountainous with indifferent roads and rough tracks needing continuous maintenance as a consequence of the severe weather. In the flatter areas tracks had often had to be marked out by slats of wire in seas of mud.

Weather conditions greatly affected operations. In autumn and winter north winds could blow blizzards lasting two or three days with heavy rain or snowfalls. Much of the mountain area was treeless, with an absence of shelter. In the summer heat could be semi-tropical; in all seasons it was very humid and liable to changes from extreme heat to cold within a very few days. Mule lines came to be protected by brushwood screens to protect animals against the wind. Minor wounds and injuries would be treated by a non-commissioned officer, some Army Veterinary Corps trained, others not but doing their best.

Exact numbers of mules participating in the three-year campaign will never be known but is thought to be about 50,000, each of the six British divisions had at any one time some 3,900 mules, with further numbers serving in army corps level units lines of communication duties. For service as muleteers 2,100 men were recruited in Greece and 4,700 were brought in from Cyprus and Malta. Many needed basic training. Sea journeys for men and mules alike remained dangerous. On 21st January 1916 only 600 out of the 1,100 mules aboard a torpedoed transport ship outside *Salonika* could be saved. In this theatre mules were indispensable, their chief roles being pulling carts and reaching gun positions in the hills. As rain and snow often made road and track conditions extremely difficult, with mules up to their stomachs in mud, it might require ten or even twelve mules for pulling instead of the usual six. Summer heat was equally difficult, with water having to be brought up to forward units. Mule packs and supply columns were frequently shelled or bombed in air raids, on some occasions Austrian artillery used poison gas. Most movements had to be at night. In the early months of the campaign the supply urgency was such that mules arriving in forward camps in the morning without rest or even pause would be set to pulling carts in the afternoon.

The campaign opened on 9th October 1915 when French and British troops disembarked at Salonika, but following

Bulgaria's entry into the war on the side of the Central Powers little could be done to help Serbia whose defeated army had instead to be evacuated by sea in the Adriatic. For the first five months of the next year the Allied forces were contained in the Salonika area, but in early 1917 they were able to move into the south of Macedonia and the south of Serbia. In June 1917 after regime changes Greece entered the war on the Allies side. In July 1918 under improved and inspired French leadership an offensive opened taking Skopje in September and advancing further into Serbia until the November armistice.

The mountain terrain, in addition to combat and logistic difficulties provided the Allies, soldiers and animals, with one disease equally serious to both. In particular in the months between May and September, continual attacks from swarms of mosquitos brought malaria, striking soldiers again and again and later to recur during the rest of their lives. In early 1917 the 600,000-strong force had been reduced to 100,000 effectives.

For mules, mange in all its forms was an especial cause of suffering during the first winter. The animals had arrived unclipped and the supply of clipping machines had broken down. Of necessity, mules had had to be put to work in heavy rain and, then wet through, to be chilled to the bone by cutting winds – to which their sensible reply was to turn round, backs to the gale. In the words of the *Official Veterinary History* "… they seemed to shrivel up and rapidly lose flesh until they were reduced to living skeletons"; the mules suffered even more than the horses. A further major cause of suffering, again especially in the early months, was a result of hay shortage. As at Gallipoli mules ate sand to provide bulk and then suffered from colic. The arrival of barley, uncooked, was to have the same result.

Mules became debilitated, especially when less fit reserve base animals were set to work. Regular exercise suited to mules was generally not feasible, though the practice of allowing them to wander freely for a few hours helped and enabled them to digest their grain ration, particularly when in the last advance stage of the campaign rations of grain were halved and hay down reduced to one quarter. A number of mules also came to suffer from glanders and other diseases. Drinking places on the roads with polluted water was a further health danger.

An initial veterinary hospital was soon followed by three more, but in early 1918 two were withdrawn hurriedly to France. Notes in the *Official Veterinary History* on the work of these hospitals record the care and treatment provided for horses, who were clearly given priority. Six small veterinary sections provided the better service for mules that were injured or sick.

Alan Wakefield and Simon Moody, joint authors of a book *Under the Devil's Eye*, give an exceptionally perceptive account of the campaign based on diaries; in respect of the daily duties and life of mules, they were, in the authors' words, "the unsung hero" of the campaign. The authors record cases of mules being drowned in heavy flooding; occasions when operational plans had to be modified or abandoned because there were insufficient numbers of mules to hand for the delivery of stores and ammunitions; the vital importance in all seasons of the delivery of water bottles to soldiers in the front line and, in cold weather, the delivery of ground sheets and blankets. From the start of the campaign mules created an unusual and unexpected problem with telephone line cables. If the necessary poles had not arrived or the ground was too hard to dig them in, wire cables had to be laid out flat on the ground where at night mules would kick them to pieces. Extra soldier guards had to be posted to protect them, but mules would then kick out at the soldiers' legs. In 1917 when the U-Boat threat was at its most dangerous, soldiers and mules were put to work in certain areas to grow a variety of vegetables; each soldier had two mules, one hour's work and two hours off. The authors also recount the generally indispensable role of the mules in casualty evacuation including the traditional forms used in the 19th century. One in the authors' words was a "sledge like contraption" mounted on side poles on which the wounded man and his stretcher were slung and then harnessed to the mule and led onwards by an orderly; the second was the Crimean War *cacolet*, two rough seats slung on either side of the mule but suitable only for casualties that could sit upright; a third was a stretcher carried on two mules walking in file; and a fourth, the least satisfactory unless roads or tracks were smooth, wheeled stretchers. Each Field Ambulance section had 120 mules.

Although no Indian Army units served in the Macedonian campaign it is clear that the experience gained in India in the 19th century played a part in reducing the hardships and suffering of this very testing theatre of the war.

Italy 1917–18

From the moment of Italy's entry into the war on 23 May 1915, the Italian Army was engaged in very stiff fighting against the army of its northern neighbour, the Austria-Hungary Empire. Much of the fighting was in steep hill and craggy mountain country. The Italian Army fought very bravely in possibly the most severe winter climate and terrain conditions of any theatre in the war. In late 1917 the Italians were being particularly hard pressed by the Austrians and requested Allied help. An Anglo-French force was sent to Italy by railway from the Western Front, the British contribution being six divisions. In March–April 1918 in view of the crisis on the Western Front two of these divisions were returned to France, the others remained in Italy until the end of the war.

Much of the historical information available relates to horses, little exists that specifically concerns the 4,000 mules at any one time supporting the British divisions. Mules arrived by rail from the south of France in open trucks, ill prepared for the winter cold of Alpine Italy and not rugged up. Food supply on their journeys was often inadequate. From rear depots the mules would be moved up to the front, often by light railway. Their role was primarily pack rather than draught cart pulling, with one soldier per mule. A training scheme was launched to prepare inexperienced animals. Much of the work was provision of supplies for the combat zone. Their general pattern of work was one of nine hours a day, in those engaged in draught cart pulling on alternate days. Loads were moved up a series of staging posts to avoid overwork or a night out on the march without shelter. They were groomed only on alternate days and for this were taken out to form a ring, all heads pointing inwards. At staging posts a Veterinary Corps dresser would test hearts and look out for sores.

At the start of the campaign regiments and battalions were allotted each twenty mules; this was soon found to be inadequate for the units' pack requirement and the number raised to forty. The mountain conditions made the work of the mule greatly valued and respected. In one, not untypical, case the mules of one battalion still at the twenty animal strength worked eighteen hours a day for eight days with very little water transporting 500 screw pickets, 600 rolls of wire, changing the 240 tins from each of 400 water dumps, all together with the other needs of the battalion – rations, tentage, 500 gallons of water per day and changes in light weapons, small arms and ammunition.

The difficulties of transport initially limited rations per mule to 4lbs of grain per day; this was found to be inadequate, reducing the mule's work capability, and the ration was raised to 15lb, including hay, per day.

Mules suffered casualties in action, mostly from Austrian air raids. Austrian aircraft dropped 'stick bombs', these exploded among the legs of animals, horses and mules, causing much suffering. Other casualties were suffered from Austrian artillery shelling, often at night and causing confusion and panic. Until

May 1918 when supplies of shoes specially made in England arrived, mules had to make do with uncomfortable local shoes, often with inadequate farrier help.

For many the very robust mules' health suffered as in Macedonia, from delayed clipping before arrival in the theatre, a delay which led to mange, becoming increasingly common. Diseases, including sleeping sickness as well as others occurred from tsetse fly attacks. Veterinary services included an initial one veterinary hospital with later a second, and an A.V.C. Mobile Veterinary Section. Horses tended to be given priority. Where there was no military staff Italian local authorities would help with staging posts. But for many sick or injured mules a long and painful journey or an equally painful wait had to be endured before evacuation to a hospital or mobile section. Trains that had brought troops to the front, being empty were then often used to take animals back to the nearest Mobile Section.

After the end of the war, mules were either evacuated for sale elsewhere or sold to local Italian communities.

The British Army's contribution to the defence of Italy is often overlooked but it was of very great value to Italy at the time. The service of some 6,000 mules that had served in the testing terrain and climate conditions is almost entirely unrecorded in histories of the 1914–18 war.

Egypt and Palestine 1914–18

Egypt, technically still an Ottoman Empire province was in practice under British administration when the Ottomans declared war on 29th October 1914. Britain had a small garrison west of the Suez Canal but Ottoman forces east of the Canal and in Sinai presented an immediate threat. Australian, New Zealand and Indian regiments, including an Indian Army Mule Corps of 1,000 mules had earlier been rushed to Egypt and elderly British and French battleships opened fire on the Ottomans from the Suez Canal lakes.

In February 1915 Ottoman troops under a German general launched an offensive against the Canal which was repulsed with little difficulty. Thereafter both sides moved their troops to Gallipoli and the Canal Zone remained quiet for some time. Further west, however, a nationalist revolt against Italian rule in Libya broke out in November 1915 and soon spread into the Sollum and Mersa Matruh areas of north-west Egypt. Much of the supply of the brigade sent to secure the area was transported by sea or carried by camels, but among the column were 160 mules. The revolt lasted until March 1916; a small number of mules fell sick, mainly from digestive problems arising from polluted water and were treated locally or sent back to Veterinary Hospitals in Alexandria or Cairo. As replacements and to meet future needs a large number of mules were imported from the United States.

After the withdrawal from Gallipoli more serious operations began in Sinai in January 1916, to be joined in June 1916 by the Arab revolt in the Hejaz. The British forces strength briefly increased as the Gallipoli divisions were reorganised, then decreased following manpower calls from the Western Front, and then again began a steady increase to the impressive early 1918 total of five British and two Indian infantry divisions, two Indian cavalry divisions and two Australian and New Zealand mountain divisions, together with a small token French force of brigade size. By the end of January 1917 Sinai had been cleared, but March and April saw reverses in two battles in Gaza. Under General Allenby a third Gaza battle in October was a victory and in December Jerusalem was occupied, the capture of Jericho followed in February 1918. After delays caused by military priorities on the Western Front the British and imperial forces finally defeated the Ottomans in September and October 1918, occupying Damascus and Beirut on 1 and 2 October and

Aleppo on the 25th. On 30th October the Ottomans signed an armistice. The Allied forces, 344,800 men were now supported by 128,950 Egyptians serving as muleteers and labour (the latter very brutally treated), together with 10,847 donkeys and 43,375 mules, a total that did not reflect a considerable number of mules that had earlier been sent to support the Arab Hejaz revolt nor supplies of donkeys from Cyprus. Further *Official Veterinary History* statistics are even less useful as few distinctions in the figures are made between horses, mules and other animals.

The terrain over which the long campaign was fought produced varying challenges. While a coastal area might offer some green vegetation, inland Sinai was desert, scrub, stone hills and sand dunes, all liable to be affected by winds. The sand dunes could change to mud in heavy rain, changing the work of mules to four for each wagon. Water supply was poor, water holes frequently producing a brackish supply which animals at first refused to drink, thereby becoming less and less efficient until they were grudgingly obliged to drink it. In many holes water remained saline and in the dry season lasting to the end of November there was frequently no water, pure or brackish, in the holes at all. Transported bottled water was then crucial. In summer the heat and khamsin winds became extreme, especially in May and June. A slow walk was the best that could be expected from man and animal. Clipping of manes and tails had to be forbidden as mules used their tails as a fan. The most important transport animal in these conditions was often the baggage camel, an animal that frightened the mules they were working with, who would then panic, creating friction among transport staff and administrative delivery problems.

Palestine, when it was entered in late 1917, presented much easier terrain – above all, it provided green vegetation on which mules and donkeys could graze. But on occasions the Palestine weather could turn bitterly cold necessitating a ban on clipping. When the ban was lifted, mange was frequently revealed in a condition that might have been observed and treated earlier. From Gaza onwards roads became muddy, creating difficulties for camels who would break their legs in frustration. 2,000 donkeys had to be brought forward urgently. A number of Ottoman army mules were captured at Jericho, all very unfit with the worst so ill that they had to be shot.

Formal ration scales for mules and donkeys were set out but frequently not be met for climate or operational reasons. A basic 8lbs of barley and 10lbs of Indian grass hay forage as it became available was authorised, to save weight and therefore transport a compressed ration of crushed barley, maize and salt was devised and issued when available. The larger American varieties of mules rejected the often poor quality Indian hay, which necessitated their replacement by a greater number of smaller mules pulling carts, four instead of the usual two. In practice this proved to be saving in efficiency, the reason probably being the clear superiority of the mules and muleteers of the Indian Army Transport Corps. Other mules arriving from India and elsewhere were unshod, creating a delay before they could be put to use; many arriving from Egypt developed conjunctivitis, requiring the issue of eye fringes. Mules from the United States were found to be suffering from glanders and ringworm, at times creating a serious difficulty. Nevertheless the health and stamina record of mules of all types remained much superior to that of horses and camels. A number of mules were killed in action, especially in 1916 and the first two battles of Gaza.

In the exceedingly difficult conditions of the campaign veterinary services could not possibly cope with the variety of problems, especially those of the camels. Services were developed as far as they could be and by the end of 1916 there were five veterinary hospitals with divisional mobile sections and depots at work. The *Official Veterinary History* records large numbers of animals treated and restored to health or sent back for convalescence, but unfortunately the totals did not distinguish between horses and mules.

The long Egypt-Palestine campaign was one of extremely testing and severe conditions for men of all continents and animals of all types and breeds. In the campaign mules had played a very valuable part in the ultimate success.

Mesopotamia and Persia

Mesopotamia was the province of the Ottoman Empire that was later to form the great part of post-First World War Iraq. Following the entry of the Ottoman Empire into the war the province became a war zone, and one of great concern to the British Empire, as the rapidly increasing British needs for oil were at the time centred in Iran, then Persia, a short distance across the Mesopotamian border. The province's most important feature was the two very large rivers Euphrates and Tigris running from Ottoman Anatolia southward across the whole land to join up and then flow into the Persian Gulf. Much of the terrain in the south and centre of Mesopotamia is a sandy, treeless plain, devoid even of stones and except near the banks of the great rivers and tributaries largely barren. North of Baghdad the ground becomes more rocky leading on to mountains in the north around Kirkuk and Mosul.

In the April to October summer months the climate is one of extreme heat worsened by burning dust-loaded winds, leaving the ground as hard-baked mud. At other times of the year rainfall can create seas of glutinous mud so deep that in some cases the extrication of trapped animals, especially mules was not possible, the animals fated to receive a bullet. In the summer flies and mosquitos abounded, bringing malaria to humans while disease in various forms, glanders, fevers, anthrax and other diseases added to the suffering of exhausted animals.

British and Indian Army units arrived in south Mesopotamia at Basra immediately after the entry of the Ottomans into the war. Ottoman attacks on the landings were repulsed and a system of barges and pontoon quays developed in the rivers for the unloading and provision of stores of forward units. Indian Transport Corps mules played an important part in this work establishing a reputation for stamina to last the whole four years' campaign. Shortages of manpower and the enormous difficulties of climate and terrain prevented any major attack upon the Ottomans until 1916. Even by the generally poor standards of the time, the administrative procedures were unbelievably bad. The first formations, arriving in hostile garrisoned land had only a very few handcarts for the transport of wounded. Local mules and other animals were hurriedly recruited. By early November 1,120 mules, the majority pack had been landed and were at work wading or swimming alongside and pushing carts along the swollen rivers, Ottoman artillery fire wounding a number. After the arrival of further brigades and supplies an ill-advised, under-strength but over-confident offensive was launched on 20th November. The assault force, some 12,000 Indian and British infantry soldiers, 1,000 cavalry, machine gun units and artillery advanced up the Tigris with the aim of taking Baghdad. Their advance was checked by a superior and well commanded Ottoman force and a number of units were forced to withdraw into the riverbank township of Kut-al-Amara where it was besieged from 3 December until 29th April 1916. The story of the five-month siege was one of extreme suffering and death for soldiers and mules alike. The rations for both were progressively reduced as food stocks ran out and attempts to relieve the garrison by boat, ground forces and, for the first time in history, air-drops of food all failed. By mid-April the British soldiers' daily ration was 1lb of meat, mule or horse, and ⅓ of an ounce of ginger. Fifteen fit mules a day were being killed for food, others suffering from non-infectious illness or injured were also shot when available. Soldiers became unable to walk, animals still alive were reduced to skeletons, with many dying. At the surrender the mules who were still struggling to survive on a diet of other mule flesh and, if available, bran, were all slaughtered to prevent their falling into use by the victorious Ottomans. Of the 18,000 mules used by the regiment in the November, attack only six survived. The disaster of Kut-al-Amara was as horrific for the mules as much as the men.

Thereafter the fortunes of the campaign steadily improved. By the end of 1916 the British and Indian force total had reached seven divisions, two cavalry brigades and artillery. A field veterinary hospital was also now available. Advance into Mesopotamia was resumed and Baghdad was captured in March 1917. Mosul and Kirkuk had been taken by the end of May 1918 and contact with Russian forces moving south from Armenia and Azerbaijan made. The port at Basra and river supply transport had been developed with improved wharfs and jetties for the mule transport onwards. The value of mule supply arrangements was again proved when regiments began to enter the mountain areas of the North-East. Although motor transport was arriving for many transport and ambulance needs, large numbers of mules, including a number captured from the Ottomans, remained in service until the end of the war. Their work continued to include supply for forward units, forty-two mules being killed in operations near Tikrit as late as October 1918.

Divisional Mobile Veterinary Sections became available and a complete veterinary hospital opened at Baghdad to which animals were transported from five forward railheads. In the extreme summer weather in central Mesopotamia sura, an anaemic and paralysing respiratory condition, and piroplasmosis struck many mules, often as a result of food shortage. Exhaustion and debility affected very large numbers.

Linked to the Mesopotamia campaign and for the same

reason, security of the oil supply, small-scale operations followed in Persia that lasted until 1921–22. A small force that came to be called the "South Persia Rifles" had landed at Bandar Abbas, on the Straits of Hormuz in 1917; the force came to be composed of a local mix of Indian Army personnel and locally recruited Persian officers and men, all under British officers. Transport for this force was horses and mules, the latter locally recruited of small size and bad physique. Many that were not shod who ran into trouble on long marches to Shiraz or elsewhere, and even those with Persian shoeing, had difficulties with cleaning. Many, small and larger, suffered pain and lameness on long marches. A small veterinary staff with a field veterinary section was attached to this force but as it was not in combat with the Ottomans it was on a low priority for equipment and stores.

North Russia 1918–1919

The 1917 Russian revolutions had led to Russia's withdrawal from the war and the turning of Communist hostility towards the Allies. In particular there was serious concern that the Soviets, at that time in control in Finland, would send submarines (in parts for reassembly) to the Kola Bay in north Russia, so threatening Allied sea routes to Murmansk and Archangel where anti-Communist forces, together with Allied ground troops, were still fighting. The Allied force had been sent to Murmansk in June 1918 and from there had moved on to Archangel; at its greatest extent, the force was holding some 400 miles of coastline. As the Arctic winter approached transport turned chiefly to reindeer and pony sledges. When in 1919 the thaw began, pack mules, transported on an existing railway line, were used for the shorter journeys to take food and supplies to forward units advancing southwards. A few carried packs, most were used to pull sledges.

A total of 771 mules had been imported for operations in North Russia. They found the bogs and mud of the thaw particularly difficult. Many floundered and sank deeper into the bogs, a number could not be extricated and had to be shot; others drowned while swimming across rivers. The overall shortages of transport often prevented the provision of mules' oat rations, their physical condition and fitness suffered. A number also were struck by a paralysis condition caused apparently by a local Archangel grass. Local Russian ponies were brought in to replace mules when they could be found.

The intervention of the Allied force became increasingly unreal, the German submarine menace ending with the November 1918 Armistice and the longer anti-Communist aims having no hope of success. The force was accordingly withdrawn in October and November 1919. None of the mules were brought back to Britain.

6

The Years Between the Wars

Mules were to figure in large numbers only on India's northern and western borders and in Iraq in the twenty-year interval between the two World Wars. In all except remote mountain conditions the motor vehicle was replacing mules and other animals in open country and cities, the stages for the increasing number and strength of the many nationalist local and territory-wide insurrections. One major consequence of this change was the possibility of a future war requiring large numbers of mules was never considered. The more able theorists saw future wars to be fast moving, the more conservative gloomily planned for a little changed return to the trenches.

Technology advances in the British and Indian armies reflected the needs of the period. Although the British Army had changed almost all of its cavalry and artillery regiments to motor power, the armoured fighting vehicles in India were too few and too poorly armed. The Indian Army did rather better, the 1918 version of the screw-gun for mountain regiments was to prove a very real field asset in Indian operations – and later in the Second World War Italian mountains. The 1918 3.7 inch Howitzer fired a 20lb shell in ranges up to 6,000 yards, if necessary over a mountain top to burst on the reverse slope, to be especially effective with shrapnel shells. A mountain regiment, one of the Indian Army's proudest elites, comprised four batteries, divided into four sections each of one gun. For the section eight mules would be needed to carry the different component parts of the gun, wheels, breech, cradle, pivot, carriage chase, trail legs and shield. Twenty-four more mules followed with ammunition, and thirty-six more for relief change-overs and more equipment. Mules and gunner drivers were given hard and thorough training. Parts of the gun were shown to the mule with a tempting morsel, perhaps a bunch of lucerne grass. The parts of the gun would then be placed on a special harness on the mule in training sequences lasting several months. If time permitted new battery mules might have to serve six months or even a year before being accepted for a gun line. With well-trained men and practised gunners, the weapon could be unloaded, assembled and ready to fire in less than a minute. The mules quickly learnt their own part of the gun and the role they should play and after firing moved back to their correct positions in the line. On the march the heavy "top loads" on the mules' backs might cause difficulties, pushing the mule forward too fast and losing control. Gunner drivers would then hang on to the mules' tails.

Almost as important new military assets but not mountain battery weaponry were the Stokes mortar and the Lewis machine gun, brought rapidly to a front line by motor transport but requiring mules for close-contact or protection work.

The second technological advance, one in signals, still required a number of mules but when motor transport could not operate, horses or camels often took pride of place with mules in a pack equipment carrying role. The disadvantages of line cable communication became even clearer as in the late 1920s and early 1930s wireless signalling became more available. Wireless equipment, especially generators was very heavy and mules appeared very slow when rapid movement

Fig. 7 3.7 Inch Mountain Battery Gun-Howitzer 1918–1945 – the wheels
mule (courtesy IWM)

was needed. Camels could carry a heavier and more fragile load safely and faster, carried their own water and did not, like the mules, require a night's rest. Signals units, therefore, came to have mixed animals. On some operations when camels were not to hand mules had to be given special training for the safe carriage of heavier loads. Mules objecting to this training were given "extra drill", carrying an extra load of sandbags across their backs. A special pack, called a Yakdan was devised for mules and ponies based on a pack harness to include two side containers to carry 80lbs each, together with one further of 20lbs for the mule's back. A small carriage pulled by two mules was used for a variety of purposes, including one with driver and especially comfortable seating arrangements known as "The Staff Car" for senior officers.

The third new development was air power, elderly aircraft of the Royal Air Force providing firepower by bombs and machine guns with great effect, providing terrain and weather conditions permitted.

Veterinary services were improved. In India graduates of Indian veterinary schools were recruited to serve as Assistant Veterinary Officers in the Indian Army. These were joined by a number of British graduate officers with later in the 1930s fully qualified Indian graduates. Thirteen field veterinary sections came to be created, with also a number of veterinary hospitals of different sizes.

India 1919–39

In Europe the only British Army involvement of mules was the despatch of four batteries of mountain artillery, sent to Chanak in 1922 at the time of the Chanak Crisis in Turkey. The batteries were at reduced strength with each gun to be pulled in draught by two mules.

India faced a series of challenges immediately after the end of the war. The first arose from an Afghan invasion, leading to the Third Afghan War of 1919–20. British policy aimed at support for a nominally independent client state of Afghanistan serving as a buffer between Russia and the British Empire of India, the state to receive British subsidy support so long as it remained friendly. This policy became challenged in February 1919 when a new Afghan king, Amanullah, came to power in Kabul after murdering his father. Believing military prowess was the only way to secure his position and extend his kingdom into India, Amanullah assembled an army of 31 infantry and seven cavalry regiments and some obsolete artillery, an army of men of ferocious bravery but poor leadership and training; with this force he launched an invasion, now generally known as the Third Afghan War, on 3rd May. He was able to draw on the support of many local tribal communities and deserters from the local Frontier Force Rifles units as he advanced. Amanullah's ambitions extended to taking Peshawar, Waziristan, Quetta and Baluchistan, with fortune including Karachi. Opposed to him was an impressive total of Indian and British regiments: 340,000 men including local regional irregulars, together with 158,000 animals, including two draught and thirteen pack mule corps. The large overall majority would have been mules. The initial operations were conventional, even at times trench warfare in style, the field artillery's 2.75-inch gun and the mountain batteries 3.7-inch howitzers playing a lead role. Amanullah's advance was checked, an armistice was signed on 3rd June with a peace treaty to follow on 8th August. In November a Mahsud uprising in Waziristan broke out. An eight-battalion force with four mountain batteries and an additional 4.5 howitzer field artillery section, all supported by 1,400 mules, was sent to the area for a four-month campaign fought in winds known as the 'breath of death'. Smaller scale guerrilla operations continued in Waziristan and Baluchistan for two more years, all requiring protected supply columns of mules. On at least two occasions Wazir and Mahsud guerrillas attacked columns with success, causing a mule panic stampede in all directions leading to the killing of soldiers and muleteers and, at best, a change of owner for the mule if still unwounded.

From 1923 onwards firmer established military control of Waziristan and Baluchistan became established by the control of a number of larger defended forts. From these regiments could and did sally forth in impressive columns up to five miles in length with as many as 2,300 mules to suppress any local violence or generally show a military presence. The forts varied in size, the biggest, Razmak in Waziristan, some 7,200 feet above sea level, normally carried a garrison of six battalions, four mountain artillery batteries, parts for regiments' motor and mule, bullock or camel transport, a veterinary hospital and other services. The most important fort on the Khyber Pass had a garrison of six battalions and a mountain battery with their support animals; other smaller forts were garrisoned by one or two regiments. To and from all these mules or donkeys were continually on the move in the long columns which would include not only subsistence supplies for the Fort's combat battalions and batteries but also the new signals companies, bakery and butchery sections, a small hospital, sanitary sections, a Veterinary Section, messes and labour sections. The mules were posted to the forts and with their specially trained muleteers allocated to regiments for that regiment's stay in the fort and posted to the next regiment at times of change-over.

The system of forts and column marches served to reduce the North-West Frontier area and Waziristan to a measure of order until the 1930s but intermittent local guerrilla style Waziri and Mahsud attacks, particularly in the transport and patrol columns with mules continued, intensifying in the Peshawar area from 1930.

In late 1936 a new major insurgency started to appear in

Waziristan, under the leadership of a local Wazir chieftain, the Fakir of Ipi. The Fakir inspired followers into horrific acts of torture and cruelty. His followers steadily grew in number in the mid-1930s requiring a force including locally recruited Scouts of over 50,000 men to contain even when using armoured cars, aircraft, artillery and machine guns.

Despite these new weaponry and aircraft assets, mules continued to play an important part. Missouri mules carried loads of over 350lbs of mountain battery screw guns at five to six miles per hour over mountainous territory, others were carrying infantry battalions' twelve Vickers-Berthier or Lewis machine guns, ammunition or subsistence supplies, and some were accompanying infantry companies and platoons in front-line service and pursuit columns. A number were killed in clashes, others by hostile snipers in ambushes at all stages of the operations.

By 1938 the scale of operations had lessened, the Fakir of Ipi had disappeared and Wazir and Mahsud insurgents having suffered heavy casualties, lost much of their enthusiasm. Nevertheless twenty-four Indian Army mountain batteries were posted to the North-West Frontier. If never entirely quiet, north-west India was not a major concern throughout the Second World War years.

Elsewhere in India unrest, sometimes violent with serious rioting and disorder, took place throughout the 1930s. The action was generally in cities, towns, peri-urban areas and plains; there when army transport was needed lorries and vans were to hand and in greatly improved quality. A few exceptions occurred, mules were used for supply needs in the 1921 south-west India Moplah uprising and again in Burma in the 1930s, but mules and other animal transport was seen as more appropriate for semi-regular or irregular forces, Scouts and Levies than for an army at war. The official total number of mules held on the government's strength dropped from 31,272 in 1921/22 to 26,194 in 1939/40. These figures will not have included mules serving in the small armies of the larger princely states permitted to have their own local field forces, nor with the totals have included the mules serving with the semi-regular Frontier Force Rifles, such as the Khyber Rifles. The quality and fitness of mules in both of these forces will have varied very greatly.

The Indian Army's transport service cadre system did however provide for a rapid expansion when needed. This was to be the case in 1940–42.

Iraq 1920–21

The second serious challenge to British imperial authority that was to involve large numbers of mules occurred in Mesopotamia. The collapse of the Ottoman Empire had released the competing ambitions and sharply differing beliefs that existed among ethnic communities from south Yemen to Turkish Anatolia, together with a jealousy, at times sharp, between Great Britain and France. The British solution for the two Ottoman Mesopotamian provinces of Basra and Baghdad was to link them with a third province, Mosul, and create a League of Nations Mandate State under an Arabian peninsula Sunni Moslem prince as King of Iraq; the state was to be very much linked to Britain as the mandatory power and after, later, independence.

In the intense 125° heat of June 1920 revolts broke out, centring on the Shia south of Iraq but also with incidents in the Kurd areas in the north-east. At the start of the rising British forces were limited, seven battalions with cavalry and artillery. The growth in popular support and action for the insurgents was progressively to increase British forces to three divisions including twenty-three British and Indian Army battalions, eight field and nine pack artillery batteries, the latter being mule, armoured cars and machine gun units and three Royal Air Force squadrons.

The arriving Indian units were accompanied by Indian mule companies, other mules were requisitioned or purchased for the different relief columns. The most important column, advancing up the Euphrates, moved in a diamond formation: with a battalion at each point of the diamond, the cavalry providing flank screens and an advance guard with supplies, pack and draught mules in the centre; water supply was crucial. Other smaller columns followed the same diamond pattern. With these and a system of some fifty fortified blockhouses with garrisons, of 100 to 200 men, British control was reasserted by the end of January 1921.

Iran 1921–22

The end of the Mesopotamia campaign was not, however, the end of operations for one brigade still in Iraq in 1921. The Russian Revolutions had created a second and more serious situation, as from 1918–19 it became clear that the new Russian Communist leaders were establishing contracts with nationalists in Persia. In May 1921 an Indian Army brigade, including a British battalion and artillery complete with regular Indian Army transport mules, marched 320 miles into Persia, establishing a base at Kasvin (now Qazvin) and control of the Caspian Sea port of Ezeli (now Asalu) in the north. The Russians, faced with a challenge from non-Communist Russian forces that had been cleared out of the Caucasus, abandoned their designs and the brigade was ordered to withdraw back to Iraq in April 1922. The British battalion, including 152 animals, mostly mules, completed a 460-mile return march in difficult weather and hill conditions in thirty-two days.

After the main operations in Iraq were over, security work was continued in the 1920s by the locally recruited Iraq Levies, who, under British command, were given weapons and a pack mule field artillery battery.

General

The use of mules by regular army formations and units in the inter-war years was limited. A small number were used in British Somaliland in the early 1920s and a few, together with donkeys in the 1936–39 Palestine conflict. Donkeys were taken to the scene of an action by motor transport "donvans" and pack mules used to support battalions and machine gun companies on patrol in hills. In the 1927–28 crisis in Shanghai mules brought from India serving with a British infantry battalion were used in support of the unit and to move light artillery. In the Middle East, especially in the Aden area, local chieftains under a loose British protection arrangement might use, or for an occasion hire to use, a few mules when faced with local dissent. In Britain itself the last and very proud Royal Artillery mule Light Battery with the splendid white mules was converted to motorised field artillery in 1937 and in 1938 the Army Veterinary School was closed down. So ended the custom at the conclusion of a Battery Officer Mess Guest Night of inviting the senior officer guest to ride a mule, usually with entertaining results.

7

The Second World War

The 1939 British Army had been planned on a "No animals in the next war" concept. For mules all that remained was a small training team of twenty-five animals.

Despite the Second World War being so much a conflict of armoured and mechanised forces and air operations together with motor transport, large numbers of mules were nevertheless involved in most campaigns. Their roles are set out in the different theatre sections of this chapter. All required the transport of mules by sea where conditions for mules on board ships improved but still remained far from ideal, especially when mules were required as a matter of urgency and also where some ships under a foreign flag were used as transport. A particular complication was the need to "black out" ships' lights to prevent their being seen at night. In some of the better ships mules were carried in pens and arrangements for good forage, a spell of exercises on deck, regular watering and oxygen for mules suffering from heat all provided. These were particularly necessary in Middle Eastern waters, where some mules collapsed from the heat and on at least one occasion oxygen was pumped into mules' nostrils from medical cylinders. Deaths on peaceful sea journeys were greatly reduced, but enemy action could cause havoc, the worst case being the bombing and sinking of the transport ship *Santa Cruz Valley* on 23rd April 1941 when 338 mules accommodated between decks were drowned.

1939–June 1940

At the start of the war it was believed that fighting would be centred on a new Western Front with, possibly also on operations in the South of France if Italy were to enter the war. The British Army's transport system was entirely motorised, which very soon proved inadequate for supply; the very severe 1939–1940 winter made a number of roads in France impossible for the motor vehicles of the time. To assist, the Indian Army Service Corps provided four mule companies, each of ninety-six pack and 288 draught mules, together with a field veterinary section; these were followed a little later by two companies from Cyprus.

The Soviet 30th November 1939 onslaught on Finland aroused much public sympathy for the Finns in both Great Britain and France. The sympathy was greatly strengthened by the sturdy resistance of the Finns in what came to be called "The Winter War". London and Paris agreed to assemble a joint military force to land in north Finland and then move to secure the north Norwegian port of Narvik, overtly to provide a route across Norway and Sweden to help the Finns with supplies but covertly to cut Germany's iron or supplies from Sweden. A joint military and naval force was assembled in British ports, it included a large number of mules to provide logistic support. The Norwegian and Swedish governments both rejected the project as a breach of their neutrality.

On 9th April 1940 the Germans invaded Norway and Denmark. The Norwegians although unprepared resisted and the British and French governments decided to try and secure the Norwegian port of Trondheim by making troop landings at

Andalsnes and Namsos on 17th and 18th April using the forces, ships and arrangements that had been prepared for the earlier project. The landings, including units from both armies were duly made and immediately came under intense German air attack, concentrating on ships and port facilities. At Andalsnes no mules were landed; at Namsos on 22nd April a 10,000-ton French transport ship carrying several scores of mules arrived but by then the port facilities had been badly damaged. Unloading the mules by boat could not be undertaken in the few hours of a Norwegian April night darkness. The ship had to return to Britain before daylight and the return of the Luftwaffe. The withdrawal of the now immobilised British and French forces followed a few days later.

In the chaotic events of May–June 1940 in France one of the Indian transport companies was surrounded and forced to surrender. All the other companies were ordered to abandon but not destroy their animals. The muleteers were withdrawn to Britain, some via Dunkirk, others by boat from Saint-Nazaire. After their arrival in Britain where they were very hospitably treated the Indian muleteers were issued with French mules withdrawn from Norway.

In the course of the war mules were brought into service from the usual sources, India, Cyprus, Argentina, Uruguay, Canada, South Africa, Italy and the biggest supplier, the United States which supplied 2,738 artillery mules and 441 pack mules. Some, from Texas, were retained in Britain and trained for Arctic warfare in Scotland and Wales.

East Africa 1940–41

At the time of Italy's entry into the war in June 1940 Eritrea, Ethiopia and Italian Somaliland were all under Mussolini's rule with Italian garrisons. British plans envisaged operations leading to a final attack on the Italians in their main stronghold, the Ethiopian highlands; these operations were to begin in the north from Sudan and from Kenya in the south. After an occupation of Italian Somaliland, a larger force would enter southern Ethiopia and move on to Addis Ababa in the centre. Offensives, both north and south opened in January 1941. The Italian forces, isolated, poorly equipped and with low morale at first gave ground relatively easily but fought with more determination in Ethiopia. Operations from Sudan in the north included a separate small "Gideon Force" entering North-West Ethiopia, a force composed largely of Ethiopian nationalists under British command and guidance and led by Orde Wingate. Common to the forces both north and south were the problems of supply transport, problems made the more difficult by the Italians' pre-war decision to evacuate all local transport to areas they believed they could retain. Columns advancing made use of mules and camels, but the latter found the heat and terrain very difficult; many camels fell out and died in the extremes of heat, the mules were not affected but remained in insufficient numbers. Pushed together from the north and south, the Italians linked together at Amba Alagi in April 1841 but, realising their situation was hopeless, they formally surrendered on 18th May.

The Gideon Force mules carried pack loads and, on occasions, the carriage of sick and wounded back to Sudan. Their numbers increased as motor transport broke down and camels fell sick and died, a number were found locally and others were captured from Italian regiments. The force's muleteers from Sudan had experience in the handling of mules; within the column Wingate and Haile Selassie, the Ethiopian emperor, rode on mules. Wingate was, however, already exhibiting his views on animals – to become very evident later in the war in Burma – by lighting fires under the stomachs of exhausted mules to make them return to the march.

The main battle-winning weapon of the northern force was

two excellent Indian Army divisions, largely equipped with motor transport but retaining mules in four mountain batteries and for supply the 800 mules of the two Cypriot mule companies, one of which included a unit of hinnies. These were later joined by captured Italian mules, many of whom were in poor condition. The mountain batteries had earlier been converted to mechanised transport and had hurriedly been converted back to mules using such animals as were available in Sudan. Packs were inevitably not always well fitted. After a Nile voyage on cattle barges, the mules had to make a twelve-day march across dry bush country, the one existing road being required for motor transport. On arrival at the scene of the decisive mountain battle for Keren, the mules had two or three times a day to climb up very steep hills or mountain slopes of 3,000 feet or more with mountain or field artillery ammunition, much carried in nose-bags. On a number of occasions the mules came under fire and were killed or wounded during the climbs and the battle. Victory in the battle was followed by the surrender of the Italians on 18th May.

Greece 1941

The Germans invaded Yugoslavia and Greece on 6th April 1941. The Greek Army and a British Commonwealth force fought bravely in the mountains but were inadequate in numbers and equipment, especially in air cover or support. They were soon forced to withdraw from the Greek mainland and, later, also from Crete. 800 mules were hurriedly landed in Greece, of which 200 were immediately sent up to the front, after receiving some very rudimentary training on the way. A further shipload were lost in the *Santa Cruz Valley* disaster; the very few survivors that had been fortunate in being released in time arrived on shore so weak and exhausted that they had to be destroyed. The constant German air attacks on ships, killing many soldiers, made it impossible to evacuate the mules that had been used in the fighting.

Syria 1941

British, Commonwealth and a small Free French contingent occupied Syria and Lebanon in June–July 1941. The occupying forces had, however, to deal with local pro-Axis contingents attacking the Allied presence in Syria, Lebanon, Iraq and Iran. The number of units that could be spared for this role was limited, especially with the ascendancy of the German Afrika Korps in Libya and in Egypt. German propaganda was proclaiming that British control in the Middle East was collapsing. In and around Tripoli (Lebanon) four mule companies were used to provide a show of force parading as "cavalry units". Ten men from the pack of three companies were issued with sword and rifle with men from the fourth being restricted to rifles only; these were then sent on show marches, some over 150 miles long.

By the end of 1942 there were some 9,600 mules in the Middle East serving in six Cypriot pack transport companies, fifteen Royal Indian Army Service Corps companies and an Indian Army mountain battery. They were soon to be needed – urgently.

North Africa 1942–43

The desert fighting in Egypt and Libya between June 1940 and December 1942 was all motor vehicle supplied. By the end of 1942, after the battle of Alamein and the Allied landings in Algeria, the terrain changed; mules, it seems largely unexpectedly, were required and were to remain an important part of transport and supply until the end of the war in 1945. The operations that followed in North Africa and Sicily were American-led, with at least half of the land forces being American. This work can only cover the operations of the very wide variety of formations and units, British, Commonwealth and Allied under British Army command.

Planning for operations in Algeria and Tunisia involving the British 1st Army landing in Algeria and the 8th Army reaching the Tunisia-Libya border had been thin. It had been based on the inclusion of the cadres of just two pack mule companies, each of 308 mules, in the Algiers landing and an expectation of, if necessary, the requisition of civilian or French military mules in the region. In the event the condition of the several thousand local mules was so poor that only 922 were obtained. These provided animals for four transport companies, a total inadequate for the operational needs in difficult terrain. Their services were nevertheless put to especially good use in support of American as well as British forces by the two companies at work in the Tunisian inland mountain area during the first five months of 1943. In this final stage of the campaign, fought in difficult scrub country after heavy rain, pack mules supplied food and ammunition to forward infantry and tank companies, special force units and, equally important, casualty evacuation using backpack litters and cacolets. An improvised veterinary service was later established for sick and injured mules and other animals.

On 12th May 1943 German resistance in Tunisia finally ceased.

Sicily 1943

British and American forces invaded Sicily on the night of 9th–10th July 1943. The American 7th Army on the south-central coast was tasked to sweep westwards to clear the western half of the island and then move north to take the island's capital, Palermo. The British 8th Army had the more difficult task of advancing up the east coast, the terrain quickly becoming mountainous. The area was stoutly defended by German and Italian troops and at the outset the weather was stormy.

German and Italian forces counter-attacked two days after the landings. The 8th Army was held in check south of Catania. The Americans, meeting less resistance, were able to reach the north-west coast and turn eastwards to help the British. On the 23rd, the two-pronged advance, from the south and from the west both heading for Messina, opened. The Germans and the Italians were forced to withdraw and plan an evacuation to the Italian mainland. By 17th August the whole island had been cleared of Axis troops.

Neither the British nor the Americans had made proper preparations for the difficult mountain areas of Sicily. The Americans had hoped, it seems somewhat vaguely, that they could requisition local mules on the island or use mules captured from Italian regiments. In similar optimism the British had included only the cadres of two mule transport companies in their landings. The local Sicilian mules, at first, were mostly found to be in poor condition, worsened by mange and poor care; the fittest had been recruited earlier by the Germans. In addition saddle-pack equipment did not fit well, creating sores as the mules were unused to them. Many also required to be shod before they could be expected to work efficiently in the mountain areas. Conditioning of the more fit animals began, fortunately, with forage and water in abundance. When restored to fitness the mules often carried not only supplies but also the heavy wireless sets needed for inter-unit communication in the mountains – an important new role. Muleteers were short in numbers, though some Canadian soldiers with cow-hand experience were only too delighted to act as muleteers, as were a small number of anti-fascist Italians. Such had been their state, though that one half of the 700 mules thought to be fit and requisitioned locally were soon exhausted or sick, while others had been hit by enemy fire, injured by ill-fitting harness or had simply been thrown about in the backs of motor lorries moving around the front. Only 315 were fit for further service at the end of the Sicily campaign.

Veterinary services were minimal, other priorities filling shipping space. The large numbers of mules that had been hurriedly despatched from the Middle East only arrived after the Axis withdrawal. But their presence, and the value of the whole learning experience of warfare in Italian mountains was soon to be proven.

Italy 1943–45

Hills reaching down almost to the beaches of Calabria and with mountains only a short distance inland required mules to arrive on the first day of Allied landings on the Italian mainland. The mules were transported by the Messina train ferry service ships to Reggio di Calabria and immediately landed. Six days later Allied seaborne landings were made at Salerno on the west coast and at Taranto on the "heel" of the peninsula. The Allied forces were then deployed with the United States 5th Army on the west coast and the British 8th Army on the east. As the twenty–month long campaign developed, soldiers from a very wide spread of continents and countries arrived to serve with or in both armies; formations and units being frequently moved across from one army to the other. Specialist mountain batteries and units were in particular demand in times of crisis.

Throughout the campaign planning for particular needs, animal administration and veterinary services were on a "common pool" basis. Estimates of future needs were made in

December 1943 when already some 10,000 soldiers were at work in the forces of all the nations involved. By this time it was already clear that a tough campaign lay ahead; planning accordingly envisaged that a permanent requirement might be 13,000 mules with a replacement rate of 1,000 per month plus an especial further 3,000 for mountain artillery support. Shipping priorities were changed from motor transport to mules, the Apennines were already dictating the nature of much of the campaign.

As a matter of urgency mules were shipped, usually to Bari on the Adriatic, from Iran, Iraq, Syria, Palestine, Lebanon, Tunisia and Cyprus. The ships so used were not prepared for

Fig. 8 Supplies for the 4th Indian Division, Italy, 1944
(courtesy IWM)

animal transport and with voyages lasting two weeks or more much hardship was imposed on the mules. Shortages of food and water, sudden storms, Arab muleteers incapacitated by seasickness, little or no opportunity for a proper leg stretch on deck all caused many casualties, a number fatal. In Italy they were joined by mules requisitioned locally, an average of 500 per month in late 1943 and early 1944. For some payment was made, prices ranging from £135 to £150 per mule. In 1944-45 6,770 mules were purchased in Sicily with a further 3,727 in Italy. By the spring of 1944 there were, in the field in Italy, seven Indian Army transport companies most with excellent Gurkha muleteers, four North African, five Cypriot, six Italian and eight French Armée d'Afrique mule companies; in total there were over 10,000 animals almost entirely comprised of mules. In the summer these were reinforced by five further Indian, two North African and five Cypriot companies. In addition and to prove of especial importance there had arrived six specially trained British Royal Artillery Mountain Batteries whose mortars and 3.7 inch howitzers or American 75mm equivalents were essential for shooting over and beyond the summits of mountains. In three of these batteries the muleteers were experienced Italian Alpine soldiers who sang irreverent Italian songs on the march, their tunes and words taken up by the British gunners. The muleteers in the other three batteries were from Basutoland (now Lesotho) whose preferred music was ritual chanting in rhythm. Other Basutos served in some of the transport companies bringing supplies, rations and ammunition forward from a railhead to battle zone units. For many of these journeys Argentinian or American Missouri mules were preferred, especially by the mountain batteries, and all given a name. The campaign included two winters extending well into April with bitterly cold temperatures, blizzards, ice and rain. Despite these conditions the Basutos won much admiration for their cheerful good humour. When necessary light coloured mules were camouflaged to a darker brown colour.

Mules suffered considerable casualties. A number resulted from accidents, injury or death resulting from accidents when mules were inadequately secured in lorries travelling at speed over rough roads, or by slipping on a mountain path. Many others were killed by enemy fire, by walking into minefields laid by retreating Germans or by booby traps laid in deceptively attractive grazing areas, or packed in bundles of forage left by roadsides. On one occasion twelve mules were killed in one minefield in one evening. A wastage rate in a major operation was assessed as 10 per cent among the regular military mule transport companies and 17 per cent among the locally recruited Italian units.

By early October 1943 Allied advances had cleared German forces out of much of Southern Italy. Naples had been occupied on 2nd October and Foggia on 27th September. On the Adriatic coast forward units had reached Termoli. Operations then slowed down, partly from sheer exhaustion and the onset of bitter weather and partly following the withdrawal of formations and units required for the Normandy landings. The Germans had been able to build the Gustav Line, a very strong defensive system based on mountain features and local rivers. In the centre stood the stoutly defended German mountain fortress of the Monte Cassino Monastery.

There followed the three battles of Cassino, the First of 12th February 1944, the Second between 15th and 18th February and the Third between March 15th and 23rd, all ending in the failure of Allied forces to take the fortress, failures involving heavy casualties and the deaths in action of many mules. The battles were fought in short daylight hours, in bitter cold, snow and ice, over the terrain of precipitous heights, narrow gorges and goat track paths that surrounded the fortress whose artillery, mortars and machine guns covered with well-directed fire. In the spring ice was replaced by thick mud as the Germans blew up weak river dams. Mules were essential, but insufficient in number; an additional problem was that mules newly arrived from remount centres were not always fully trained in pack work. If it happened there were no mules available units would have no choice but to withdraw, having no ammunition. For basic needs such as water or mortar bombs, grenades and rifle ammunition mules might have to make a series or more of mountain treks, sometimes losing several animals and their loads on the way as the Luftwaffe made continuous bombing and machine gun attacks on mule columns. On their return journeys mules carried casualties – and dead bodies. A number of wounded were carried in Crimean War style cacolets. Of Cassino the historian Fred Majdalany, himself a veteran of the campaign later wrote:

"The army that could call on 600 tanks, 400 aeroplanes and 60–70,000 vehicles of all shapes and sizes found itself dependent on the humble pack mule. In the mountains above Cassino in February, a mule was worth a dozen tanks."

Reorganisation of the Allied armies and improved weather conditions enabled a final assault beginning on 17th May to bring success with the capture of the fortress by Polish troops. This assault was part of a wider offensive that liberated Rome and in the summer months reached the Arno River. By the end of August Pisa, Florence and on the coast Rimini had all been liberated. Throughout this advance mule companies had continued to play an essential role in central Apennine Mountains and hills, but still also continuing to suffer losses of muleteers and mules. The Allied advance was brought to a halt south of Bologna, the Germans constructing a further strong defensive system, the Gothic Line, south of the Po River and so forcing a second winter campaign on the weary Allied armies. For the mountain units, howitzers or mortar batteries operations continued to be marches through gorges sometimes only a yard or two wide, cold, sleet, rain and enemy fire. Actual fighting remained that of small platoon or company-sized sub-units advancing from one crag to the next, requiring a constant supply of small mortars, machine guns and ammunition together with the transport of heavy wireless sets. If companies were supplying Indian Army regiments their loads might include live sheep. On several occasions the mountain batteries special over-the-mountain top fire opened the way for Allied advances. Also in these months a number of mules were delivered, some by air, to the partisan forces of Marshal Tito at work on the other side of the Adriatic.

Although the winter months were to bring a lull in the intensity of the fighting the supply for forward units in carefully prepared and carefully concealed "mule heads" together with casualty evacuation had to be made at night, long men and mule columns in groups of six over the twelve hours of darkness in very heavy rain knee, sometimes waist high in liquid mud and snow, or ice which had at least the virtue of a harder surface but left mules with icicles hanging from their noses. On a number of occasions mules slipped over the edge of a narrow ridge path requiring that they, terrified by their fall, be hauled back by rope. A number of pack mules stepped on mines or nibbled at booby-trapped corn stacks to meet an unpleasant death. On only a few occasions could the daylight parts of their journey be protected against German gunfire by a smokescreen.

The Basuto muleteers remained generally cheerful. Although they accepted the need to wait for dusk or night marches they found journeys in the dark very difficult. Recreation for all, when circumstances so permitted in the early spring of 1945 included flat and jump mule racecourses with Basuto muleteers as jockeys.

In mid-April the final Allied offensive opened, soon turning into a pursuit with Genoa, Turin and Padua being liberated by the 28th and a surrender of German forces agreed on the 29th, to take effect on 2nd May.

Veterinary services for the large number of mules in the campaign had been hard to provide. Local Italian veterinary surgeons were used when available. One British veterinary hospital was at work by the end of 1944, withdrawal facilities developed when mules were no longer needed, and an American veterinary centre deployed to support the 8th Army. Animal equipment, packs, saddles and nosebags remained a problem throughout the campaign. There was never a sufficient number of farriers; Cypriots, Indians, Basutos and Italians were all trained to varying degrees of competence to fill the gaps and more satisfactorily meet basic needs of the removal of encrusted mud and clipping. The very severely damaged Italian railway system had been partially restored and motor transport had become more freely available, so enabling mules to be brought to the forward areas more quickly and sick or wounded animals to be withdrawn.

The Italian campaign was the first of the two Second World War campaigns to be epic for mules. The total number of mule casualties among all the Allied forces will never be known but in companies and batteries under British command over 600 were killed and over 1,000 wounded or injured. When the campaign ended Italian mules were returned to their former owners and the best of the imported mules were shipped off to the even worse conditions of Burma. There, fortunately for them the campaign, the second and greatest epic for mules, had only a few weeks to run.

Burma 1942–45

Burma, or to give the country its modern name Myanmar, was the scene of probably the most difficult and physically exhausting campaigns in the history of the British and Indian armies. The country combined to an extreme degree the geographic problems of mountain and jungle, a dangerously unhealthy tropical climate of extreme heat in April and May, of torrential monsoon rain from May to September when jungles became mud and rivers flooded, and a period from September to April when each month warm days became hotter but capable of producing a freezing cold early morning dew. Disease, in particular malaria and dysentery but including several others which not only killed or incapacitated many, debilitated and weakened the energies of all. To these factors must be added a determined and fanatical jungle-wise enemy, the Japanese, all at a time when metropolitan Great Britain's priorities lay in west Europe. For most of the long campaign forward line positions or groups operating behind the front line in enemy-held territory could not be supplied by motor transport. Although transport aircraft numbers increased they were never adequate for supply needs. Scores of thousands of mules, from South Africa, India, Argentina and the United States were brought to Burma after long and often distressing sea journeys, these then were entered into the fighting, suffering all the same privations as the soldiers they tried to serve. Despite the climate and terrain the loads that mules would have to carry weighed over 70lbs or more. The larger Argentinian mules would carry a heavier load and the biggest mules, American Missouris, would carry loads of 200lbs, on occasions even more. Muleteers being in short supply, one man was expected to handle three mules. With the exception of casualties all soldiers were forbidden to ride on mules.

A brief summary outline of the several phases of the campaign may help readers. Japan entered the war on 7th December 1941 at Pearl Harbour. On the following day Hong Kong was attacked. British, Canadian and Indian troops, these including the Hong Kong Mule Corps comprising four troops each of ninety mules, resisted the Japanese for seventeen days before the inevitable surrender. The mules supplied the forward units with rations, mortars, ammunition, wireless equipment and blankets; they

Fig. 9 Mules supporting the advance of Punjabi soldiers in Burma
(courtesy IWM)

also helped in the evacuation of casualties. Others were with forward surgical teams, all often under fire. In the final stage, the withdrawal from the mainland to Hong Kong Island, the lighter earmarked to carry the mules across to the island was sunk by Japanese bombers and the mules had to be abandoned. For the next several weeks Japanese priorities lay in Malaya and Indonesia, for Burma a period of frantic preparation.

Powerful Japanese offensives then opened in January and February 1942 when they launched a very strong thrust into the areas of economic importance north from Rangoon to Mandalay and beyond towards Myitkyina. From there they planned an invasion of India. Under the command of General Slim an ill-equipped Indian and British army force of two divisions conducted an epic fighting withdrawal, barring the way to India by maintaining a measure of control of regions in the Arakan mountain hills, swamps and paddy fields to the west of the Irrawaddy river and, further north across the Chindwin river, in the Imphal, Naga Hills and Kohima plains and hill areas of Manipur. In the course of the very rapid withdrawal, 400 miles in little over three weeks, large numbers of mules had to be shot as from sheer exhaustion they could no longer continue to march. Only some 1,500 arrived safely in the new defended areas. There they were joined by mules brought in by rail from across India. During their journeys, they had had to endure crowded trains, irregular food and limited water supply. Many were fractious on being unloaded from the trains, control was sometimes regained by leading a white pony in the direction the mules were required to go; the mules followed with enthusiasm. Breaking in and training then began. When completed British and Indian battalions at or near full strength were allowed twelve jeep motor vehicles and forty-one mules, with a further fifty-eight held for each battalion by the divisional Animal Transport Company. Others were sent to field medical centres and sections.

In November 1942 Indian and British forces opened an offensive in the Arakan but were not sufficiently strong to achieve success. In March 1943 the Japanese launched a counter-offensive and in May the British offensive came to an end. In these months Brigadier Wingate's First "Chindit" long range penetration column first appeared in February 1943 operating with ambushes on Japanese convoys deep in Japanese occupied jungle territory in seven columns each with seventy mules, all a little over a mile in length. The far-behind-the-enemy's-front-line special atmosphere contributed to an equally special interdependence between soldiers and the mules who appeared to sense this. But when the columns had turned about after fulfilling their mission and were on the move back to safety mules had to be shot to avoid revealing the line of march. The shootings created very great distress among officers and muleteers especially after an experiment in throat slitting in lieu of shooting, an experiment not repeated.

The second and very much larger Chindit operation including Mountain Battery artillery with screw-guns appeared in February 1944 at a time when Japanese attacks had opened in both the Arakan and Manipur regions, at Imphal in March and at Kohima in April. After desperate fighting in the worst possible jungle conditions the Japanese were defeated. In early December Slim's Indian and British 14th Army began crossing the Chindwin, mules carrying boats as well as heavy field wireless sets. At the same time an assault from the Bay of Bengal landed a fresh Indian Army division with some 2,000 mules in the Arakan.

The tide had now turned against the Japanese. In February 1945, the 14th Army began the crossing of the Irrawaddy. In one sector, alone 400 mules swam across the Irrawaddy in a morning; in the Chindwin crossing muleteers hung on to their animals' tails during the 800 yards swim. In March, Mandalay was liberated. In April, amid very heavy rainfall, the Arakan campaign ended and the port of Akyab occupied. In the next month, an assault from the sea cleared the Japanese out of Rangoon.

In one epic June 1945 march in monsoon weather an Indian Army brigade including a Mountain Artillery Regiment and over 1,000 mules had for three weeks to march over 100 miles of 6,000 feet high tangled jungle and individual hills. In one phase the daily journey required ascents and descents in six mountain ranges each of 4,000 feet in ten miles. In one area the mountain paths were only two feet wide. Mules slipped to their deaths many hundreds of feet below. One was found lodged on the top of a tree. At the bottom of the valley mules had to wade in thick mud, in some gorges raging torrents of water. Drowning mules had to be shot, many died of exhaustion. Nevertheless the very large American artillery mules still managed to carry loads of over 420lbs.

With the exception of one large-scale operation in July when the Japanese attempted a break-out to try and reach neutral Thailand the remaining operations were smaller, based on the despatch by units of platoon thirty men-sized patrols out with mules and three-day ration packs. These mopping-up operations ceased with the Japanese surrender on 14th August 1945.

Mules of the Indian army transport service and the mountain batteries were by far the largest component of the forward transport and supply services, but never in sufficient numbers. Statistics and totals during the three and a half years of the fighting are far from complete but a few figures are illustrative. In the Manipur area, including Kohima and Imphal initial deployment was based on fifteen mule transport companies each of some 470 mules. In the first Chindit operation over 900 mules carried stores ammunition and wireless sets, one man for two mules at the outset, reducing to one man for three or four as casualties mounted. No mule returned. In the second

Chindit operation 3,154 mules were involved, over 1,000 being flown in; 1,169 lost their lives. After the 1944–45 changes in fortune, between 31st March 1944 and 1st April 1945 23,595 first and second line mules together with 378 donkeys were on the strength of the South East Asia command.

A difficulty, at times serious, was the numbers of and quality of muleteers. Newly arriving Indian Army divisions had all been trained on motor transport. Muleteers, Indian, Gurkha and British, had to be trained in a hurry, the training including swimming. Some were at first not enthusiastic, others went to the other extreme, sentimentally regarding their mules as pets. Immediate arrival challenges could be disconcerting, in the Arakan Mountain Pass tracks and swollen rivers forming seas of liquid mud. Companies in the first retreats might have to move with loads some twenty-five miles a day for several days. Others, expecting action, found their first missions were provision of food for refugees. As part of their preparation for Chindit column work or other jungle operations and to avoid giving positions away by braying some 5,500 mules suffered total incision of their vocal cords in a swift surgical operation. A very small number died, but with only one or two rare exceptions all others had lost their voice for the rest of their lives. Grey mules had their coats darkened with potassium permanganate as camouflage, which was essential for jungle operations.

Supply of food for men and forage for mules on long marches together with the replacement of mule casualties by fresh animals was helped by 300 flights of air power. This took various forms, sometimes direct by the landing of aircraft, in particular the famous American Douglas C47 Dakota, sometimes by the dropping of essential stores, weapons and ammunition by parachute and on a number of occasions by the use of gliders. For the relatively simple needs of the Dakota three landing strips, Aberdeen, White City and

Broadway each in some 3,000 feet of jungle, were cleared. Each animal-carrying aircraft carried four or five small size mules together with their muleteers. In the case of the big American mules only three could be flown. Loading and unloading had generally to be done in moonlight. Unloading involved backing the mules out pulling the tails of frightened, kicking mules. In the C47s and the gliders two mules were pulled or pushed into bamboo pole stalls, bolted to the floor at the front of the aircraft, one on each side, and two more were bolted to the floor at the rear of the aircraft, so leaving an aisle down the middle. It seems that at critical times a fifth mule would be carried under improvised rope arrangements in the aisle. If the aircraft was towing gliders, an extra three mules were carried. The mules would sometimes be provided with nosebags and were generally but not always quiet, but there were flights in which mules had to be shot as they were endangering the aircraft. Not all the landings, particularly those of the gliders, were happy, mules suffering a broken leg having to be shot. There were even a few experiments made in the direct dropping of individual mules by parachute. The mules were first sedated and wrapped in protective packaging. Others were dropped directly but the jerk on the mules' harness that followed the opening of the parachute killed six mules and the whole project was abandoned.

In combat mules found small arms fire, either from Japanese ground troops or machine gun fire from aircraft, very disturbing, with panic often setting in. They were much less concerned about artillery bombardment or aircraft bombing. In one Japanese tank attack 218 mules were mown down and killed. When possible, mules were rested some distance from British or Indian guns so that if the Japanese were to target the battery the mules would survive. Mules often found difficulties with the frequent river crossing, refusing to swim when waters

Fig. 10 A reluctant mule being pushed into a Dakota C47 aircraft, Burma 1945 (courtesy IWM)

were fast flowing; they would up-turn boats and have to be dragged to the riverbank. Some officers noted an importance in keeping mules' heads above water as, if water entered their ears, mules would give up hope and effort. Limited food rationing in combat periods weakened mules' energies, although the supply of forage was whenever possible given a high priority. Day to day problems affecting mules included a very large number of buckle, saddle withers and gall sores, injuries from bamboo stumps, poisonous plants, leeches and mosquitos. Usually the treatment to hand was limited to gentian violet, this could produce a seal so enabling the mule to proceed with his work.

Disease was a major problem; in particular the paralysing respiratory Sura disease affected thousands of mules, as did anthrax. On the march apparently fit mules could very quickly become distressed and immobile and have to be destroyed. After some experiment and research packages of ampoules of antrypol were dropped from aircraft to columns on the march and they proved to be effective.

At the start of the campaign veterinary services were very limited and throughout the whole period veterinary care was constrained by the distances in the remote jungle in which the animals were at work, and the difficulties of any form of rapid ambulance transport, motor, rail or cart for the withdrawal of sick or injured animals. Treatment centres even if available were a long way away, moving mules would involve protracted journeys for which forage and water might not always be available. The existing January 1942 veterinary services were severely mauled and broken up in the retreat, but four veterinary sections and one field hospital were soon at work. In April 1942 a base hospital for which further field sections were sent out was set up in Assam with further facilities in India. A second hospital followed later but shortages of veterinary staff remained. The hospitals were rough and ready, the animal stalls made of dried grass and reeds within a bamboo framework all covered by tarpaulin roofs. Wingate's second Chindit column included veterinary sections but it was only in late 1944 and early 1945 that there were sufficient numbers of veterinary officers, full stores, field veterinary hospitals, convalescent depots and field sura units available for the expanded field army.

Overall the psychological dimension of the war in Burma was different from and larger than in other British Second World War campaigns in two respects. First the difficulties of terrain, climate, exhaustion and disease, supply shortages and the ferocity of the Japanese already noted. But second also, in part occasioned by the first but also by the virtues of energy, single-minded drive and endurance being carried to excess by one or two field commanders, in particular Orde Wingate accepting even appearing to impose, the most severe hardship and suffering. Loss of life was of course inevitable, but in the tense atmosphere of command there appeared a wider view that such losses, human and animal were on occasions the more expendable. With the wisdom of hindsight it seems clear that some operations were too hurriedly prepared and the larger losses of life unnecessary.

In these circumstances and conditions, fatigue and frustration led to frayed tempers, on occasions some soldiers and even some muleteers came to hate their mules and, under the strain, hold them in contempt rather than care. A number of newly-arrived mules had had little training in pack work; equally not all the muleteers had proper training. Mules with loads even carefully loaded, would find their loads caught on outcrops of rock and stone or bamboo clumps, levering them over the edge or slipping on a narrow track; muleteers would curse. In a few cases an uncontrolled movement by a mule would give positions away to Japanese artillery. If legs were broken the mule would be shot. If a mule was slithering about on steep grasses he might be pushed, beaten or kicked; but if a particular pathway had to be used frequently the mule might have remembered and tried to take precautions not understood by the muleteer. Before the vocal chord procedure was introduced mules would be gagged – an ungentle procedure. Various not very gentle methods were used to oblige mules to cross a river. One was to try and rush several mules into a river leaving them no option but to swim onwards, heads swaying like the heads of snakes in protest. A decoy "Judas" mule with perhaps a bell around his neck, or a mule known to be trusted by others in a group, would be towed from the back of a boat so as to lead others to follow. Sometimes a wedge-shaped corral closing at the riverbank would be hurriedly built and mules were pushed into it, again leaving no option but to enter the water, perhaps also encouraged by the well-known "feed" call of a bugler on the opposite bank. A few mules might also be hitched to the sterns of motor-powered boats or rafts which then pulled away into the river, muleteers beating and pushing their mules from behind. In withdrawals mules that were going to have to be abandoned would be shot and used to provide food for soldiers and muleteers. Many muleteers and soldiers were distressed by this, with a number refusing to eat the cooked mule meat. Most distressing of all perhaps were the occasions when the quick arrival of Japanese was expected and mules were left behind with a hand grenade loosely packed in their harness.

The passions aroused in these scenarios and many others bore heavily on the mules. The best and better muleteers were aware of the hardship. The best were devoted to and bonded with their mules, hugging them and whispering to them, giving them pet names and chatting to them on the march and in rest periods and weeping bitterly if their mule was killed or died. On occasions muleteers would carry the mule's load themselves to give their animal a respite, or give up their rations to their mules. A newly-arrived replacement muleteer, however good, might not know of the personal idiosyncrasies and fears based on experience of individual mules, how to ascertain whether an individual mule preferred to kick sideways or to kick backwards. So it is not surprising that in the conditions of Burma and lack of experience, particularly among British soldiers and some muleteers that animal welfare was often ignored. After the end of the fighting in Burma itself, 700 mules were despatched by sea to the Americans for operations in China. Over half were lost at sea. Perhaps saddest of all was that after the war many scores of mules were put down humanely in specially-built abattoirs. Others were sold off cheaply to harsh and ruthless Indian cart drivers in Calcutta or other Indian cities or towns. Only a fortunate few were retained for further service in India.

The defence of India and the liberation of Burma could not possibly have been achieved without the mule. The campaign in Burma was the mules' finest hour.

8

Operations Since 1945: Conclusion

The decades since 1945 have seen the decline but not the disappearance of the mule in the service of the British military. Improved motor transport, air transport and, from the 1950s, the helicopter completed the take-over of supply from animals except in cases of exceedingly difficult terrain or very special circumstances. British rule in India was to last only for two more years. Although British regiments and batteries were very quickly withdrawn from the north-west frontier, a few British officers remained for a very short time before handing over to officers of the Indian or future Pakistan officers. Conditions, too, had changed, the railway could reach the frontier from Bombay and mules were argued by nationalists to be out-dated symbols of British rule. Several hundred were destroyed in a specially-constructed abattoir.

In Europe a reminder of the state of the post-war continent was the use in 1945–46 of mules by the British military administration in Germany. In certain badly bombed cities under British control mules of the former German Army were used by naval and military officers to clear streets and roads from the wrecks of destroyed buildings. Mule carts sometimes replaced private vehicles as public transport or were used in rubble clearance, often revealing distressing remains.

In the major end of empire campaigns, mules and donkeys appear as a small detail on two occasions. In the Cyprus conflicts donkeys were used to supply food and equipment to battalions serving in the Troodos Mountains and Paphos forests. In June 1965, during the confrontation with Indonesia in Borneo, a pack howitzer of a field battery serving in Hong Kong together with twelve mules were used to support a Gurkha battalion in the destruction of an Indonesian machine gun post.

In the next two operations, rather greater numbers of mules were deployed; both took place in Oman, in South-East Arabia. The first was mounted from – as it then was – the Colony and Protectorate of Aden in 1958–9 and was not at first officially admitted by the British government. The issue at stake was the threat to the ruler of Oman whom Britain had long supported from a rebellion against his authoritarian rule, a rebellion supported by Saudi Arabia. The terrain held by the rebels was a mountainous plateau, the Jebel Akhdar, that could only be scaled by narrow paths. British help for the Sultan's force took the form of Special Air Service Regiment (SAS) personnel and a platoon of the Life Guards, whose food and ammunition supply was to be based on a cheap but misguided purchase of 200 small Somali donkeys; they were brought in to the combat zone by landing craft and landed five or six at a time in nets. The donkeys' load capability was only 50lbs, a shortcoming to present problems, particularly as they disliked heights and lay down if the terrain was over 1,000 feet. In 1973, on at least one occasion, donkeys with their vocal chords cut figured in the front line of an attacking unit. The donkeys were also used in deception tactics confusing rebels over attacks. In some operations, to ensure a quiet approach, hooves were covered in hessian. The revolt was quickly repressed but only to be followed by a second and more serious Marxist-inspired rebellion in the Dhofar eastern region of Oman in 1968–1974. A number of local regiments, most led by British officers and all with British Army support were involved in a five-year campaign. Transport across desert and mountain included a large number of mules for long marches, on the march columns would evacuate casualties and receive some supplies by air drop, these included forage for the mules. The campaign was a success, as there was the replacement of the old sultan with a younger and progressive ruler in 1970, which ended much of the rebels' disaffection.

Although the 1991 Kuwait War was essentially one of a quick desert and scrub armoured formation battle, in the build-up mules were to play their traditional supply column role over the long distance; these had to be covered for supplies coming from Saudi Arabia, particularly from Riyadh to the forward maintenance area. British regiments benefited from these supplies but the mules were not part of any British unit or formation.

Until 1975 mules formed a vital part of the frontier security of Hong Kong, providing the supply for the colony's garrison Gurkha battalion's periodic border patrol columns. These operations were discontinued in 1975 and the last British Army mule unit disbanded. So ended a notable historic relationship of service by an apparently unremarkable and humble animal to the British Army. The relationship should never be forgotten.

Much military history records the hardship, often privation and suffering of soldiers in the severe campaign, terrain and climate conditions of many combats. The mule also suffered these, food and water shortages, sores and disease, exhaustion, wounds and death along with their soldiers. Soldiers had frequently to pay the penalty of poor command or harsh leadership at regimental unit level, the mule too had these, often taking the form of poor, uncaring, untrained drivers and muleteers. If there is one "lesson" to be drawn from this work it is that the more care given to an animal in military service the better will be the service the animal provides. The mule is an animal of exceptional stamina, but he is also of flesh and blood, a part of Creation and deserving respect.

Increasingly when writing this work I felt a sense of obligation. I was setting out a record and it was a duty and a privilege to be doing so.

> The keen old head and the long cocked ear
> And the nostril quivering wide.
> The beamy back and quarters broad
> And these are all allied
> To a temper kind tho' oft maligned
> By some untutored fool.
> The finest Friend that God designed
> The Mountain Battery Mule.

> Colonel M. D. Bell, a mountain battery commander,
> *The Gunner*, April 1964

Published Sources

A

Anon, *The Army in India and its Evolution*, Calcutta, Government Printer, 1924

Atwood, Rodney, *The Life of Field Marshal Lord Roberts*, London, Bloomsbury Academic, 2015

Auphan, Rear Admiral Paul and Jacques Mordal, trans. Captain A.J.C. Sabalot, *The French Navy in World War II*, Annapolis, U.S.N.I. 1950

B

Beadon, Colonel R.H., *The Royal Army Service Corps*, Cambridge University Press, 1931

Bierman, John and Caroline Smith, *Fire in the Night. Wingate of Burma, Ethiopia and Zion*, London, Macmillan, 1944

Billière, General Sir Peter, *Looking For Trouble*, London, Harper Collins, 1995

Blenkinsop, Major-General Sir J. and Lieut-Colonel J.W. Rainey, *History of the Great War Based on Official Documents Veterinary Services*, London, H.M.S.O., 1935

Blight, Brigadier Gordon, *The History of the Royal Berkshire Regiment 1920–1947*, London, Staples, 1953

Bryant, Arthur, *Years of Victory*, London, Collins, 1944

Burnett, W.G., *Wingate's Phantom Army*, Bombay, Thacker, 2006

C

Carmichael, Pat, *Mountain Battery*, Bournemouth Devin, 1983

Carton de Wiart, Lieutenant-General Sir Adrian, *Happy Odyssey*, London, Jonathan Cape, 1950

Chandler, David, *Marlborough As A Military Commander*, London, Batsford, 1973

Chesney, Kellow, *Crimean War Reader*, London, Frederick Muller, 1960

Clabby, J., *The History of the Royal Army Veterinary Corps, 1919–1961*, London, John Allen, 1963

Clayton, Anthony and Donald C. Savage, *Government and Labour in Kenya 1895–1963*, London, Cass, 1974

D

Dimbleby, Richard, *The Frontiers are Green*, London, Hodder and Stoughton 1943

Duncan, Captain Francis, *History of the Royal Regiment of Artillery, Vol. II*, London, John Murray, 1873

E

Essin, Emmett M., *Shavetails and Bell Sharps, The History of the U.S. Army Mule*, Lincoln, Nebraska University Press, 1997

F

Fergusson, Bernard, *The Wild Green Earth*, London, Collins, 1947

Fleming, Peter, *Bayonets to Lhasa*, Tauris Parke, 2012

Flower-Smith, Malcolm and Edward Yorke, *Mafeking, The Story of a Siege*, Welterreden, Covos Day Books, 2000

Fortescue, John, *The Royal Army Service Corps, Vol. I*, Cambridge University Press, 1930

G

Gardiner, Juliet, *The Animals' War*, London, Portrait, 2006

Goldstein, Wilf, *Farewell Screw Gun*, Lewes, The Book Guild, 1986

H

Haldane, Lieut-General Sir Aylmer, *The Insurrection in Mesopotamia, 1920*, London, Edinburgh, William Birdwood, 1922

Harfield, Alan, *Pigeon to Packhorse*, Chippenham, Picton, 1989

Headlam, Major-General Sir John, *The History of the Royal Artillery 1860–1916*, Woolwich, Royal Artillery, 1940

Heathcote, T.A., *The Indian Army, The Garrison of British Imperial India*, London, David and Charles, 1974

Heathcote, T.A., *Mutiny and Insurgency in India, 1852–58*, Barnsley, Pen and Sword, n.a.

H.M.S.O., *Florence Nightingale and the Crimea 1954–55*, London, 2000. (First published in 1855)

I

Institution of the Royal Army Service Corps: *The Story of the Royal Army Service Corps*, London, G. Bell, 1955

J

Johnson, Malcolm K., *Yield To None, The History of the King's Own Yorkshire Light Infantry 1945–1968*, Leeds, Propagator Press, 2005

L

Lee, Albert, *History of the 33rd Foot*, Norwich, Jarrold, 1922

Lunt, James, *Imperial Sunset*, London, Macdonald, 1981

M

MacMunn, Lieut-General Sir George, *The Armies of India*, Bristol, Crecy, 1984

Majdalany, Fred, *Cassino, Portrait of a Battle*, London, Cassell, 1957

Masters, John, *The Road Past Mandalay*, London, Michael Joseph, 1961

Maurice, General Sir Frederick and others, *History of the War in South Africa, 1899–1902*, London, Hurst and Blackett, 1906

Millar, Ronald, *Kut, the Death of an Army*, London, Secker and Warburg, 1969

Moorehead, Alan, *Gallipoli*, London, Hamish Hamilton, 1926

N

Napier, Lieut-Colonel H.D., *Field Marshal Lord Napier of Magdala*, London, Edward Arnold, 1927

Nasson, Bill, *The South African War 1899–1902*, London Arnold, 1999

O

Oman, C.W.C., *Wellington's Army*, London, Edward Arnold, 1912

P

Packer, Charles, *Return to Salonika*, London, Cassell, 1964

Parkinson, Roger, *Moore of Corunna*, Abingdon, Purcell, 1976

Poynder, Lieut-Colonel F.S., *The 9th Gurkha Rifles*, London, RUSI, 1937

Pugsley, Christopher, *Gallipoli*, London, Pen and Sword, 2014

R

Redding, Tony, *War in the Wilderness*, Stroud, Spellman, 2012

Rhodes James, Robert, *Gallipoli*, London, Batsford, 1965

Robertson, Ian, *A Commanding Presence: Wellington in the Peninsula*, Stroud, Spellmount, 2008

Robson, Brian, *Crisis on the Frontier*, Stroud, Spellmount, 2007

Royal Welch Fusiliers, *White Dragon: The Royal Welch Fusiliers in Bosnia*, Wrexham, published by the Regiment, 1995

Rutter, Owen, ed., *The History of the Seventh (Service) Battalion of the Royal Sussex Regiment, 1914–1919*, London, The Times, 1934

S

Seligman, *Vidy, The Salonika Sideshow*, London, Allen and Unwin, 1919

Smith, Major-General Sir Frederick, *A History of the Royal Army Veterinary Corps 1796–1919*, London, Ballière, Tindall and Cox, 1927

Selby, John, *The Boer War*, London, Arthur Barker, 1969

Sutton, John, *Wait For the Waggon*, Barnsley, Pen and Sword, 1998

T

Takle, Patrick, *Nine Divisions in Champagne: The Second Battle of the Marne*, Barnsley, Pen and Sword, 2015

Tegetmeier, W B and C L Sutherland, *Horses, Asses, Zebras,*

Mules and Mule Breeding, London, Horace Cox, 1895

Tennant, R.J., "Wellington's Mules" article in three parts appearing in *The Mule* issues of Winter 2010, Summer 2011, Autumn 2011

Thompson, Julian, *The Imperial War Museum Book of the War in Burma, 1942–45,* London, Pan, 2003

Travis, Lorraine, *The Mule,* London, J.A. Allen, 1990

W

Wakefield, Alan and Simon Moody, *Under the Devil's Eye,* London, Sultan, 2004

War Department, *Animal Management,* London HMSO, 1934

Watteville, Hyde, *Waziristan, 1919–1920*

Wilks, John and Eileen Wilks, *The British Army in Italy, 1917–1918,* Barnsley, Leo Cooper, 1998

Woodfin, Edward C., *Camp and Combat on the Sinai and Palestine Front,* Basingstoke, Palgrave Macmillan, 2012

Woodward, David, *Forgotten Soldiers of the First World War,* London, Tempus, 2000

Wylly, Colonel H.C., *The Loyal North Lancashire Regiment, Vol. II,* Doncaster, n.d.

Y

Yorke, Edward, *Britain, Northern Rhodesia and the First World War,* Basingstoke, Palgrave Macmillan, 2013